AVATAR
Fire and Ash
THE VISUAL DICTIONARY

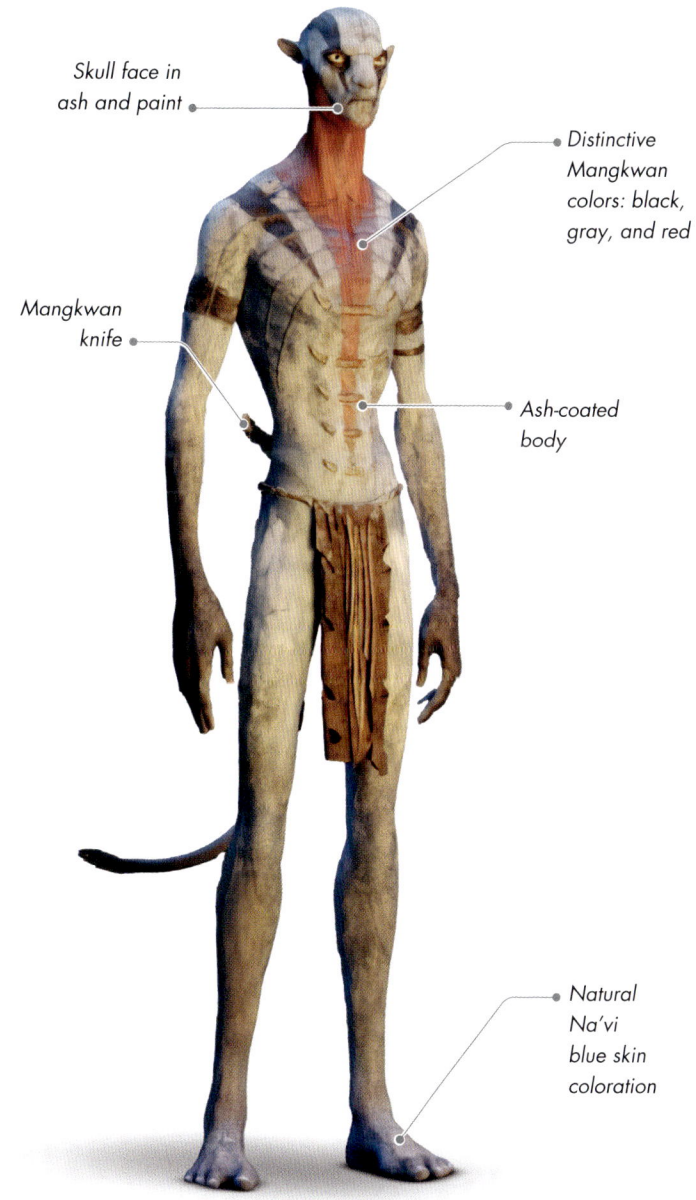

- Skull face in ash and paint
- Distinctive Mangkwan colors: black, gray, and red
- Mangkwan knife
- Ash-coated body
- Natural Na'vi blue skin coloration

MANGKWAN WARRIOR

PEYLAK

AVATAR
FIRE AND ASH

THE VISUAL DICTIONARY

BASED ON THE STORY, CHARACTERS,
AND WORLD CREATED BY

JAMES CAMERON

WRITTEN BY
Reymundo Perez

TLALIM KNIFE

BRAIDED TOP

CONTENTS

FOREWORD BY STEPHEN LANG	6
PANDORA	8
THE SULLY FAMILY	**10**
JAKE SULLY	12
NEYTIRI	14
KIRI	16
LO'AK	18
TUKTIREY	20
THE OMATIKAYA CLAN & ALLIES	**22**
OMATIKAYA LIFE	24
OMATIKAYA TOYS	25
MO'AT	26
TARSEM	27
DR. NORM SPELLMAN	28
SPIDER	30
IKEYNI	32
THE METKAYINA CLAN	**34**
METKAYINA VILLAGE LIFE	36
TONOWARI	38
RONAL	40
TSIREYA	42
AO'NUNG	44
ROTXO	45
COVE OF THE ANCESTORS	46
FLUX DEVIL	48
THE OCEAN OF PANDORA	**50**
THE TULKUN COUNCIL OF ELDERS	52
TSYONG	54
ZUKZUK	56
AKULA	57
ABOVE PANDORA	**58**
THE TLALIM CLAN	60
A WIND TRADER MARKET	62
WIND TRADERS' GONDOLA	64
SAILING THE SKYWAYS	66
WEAPONS	67
PEYLAK	68
MEDUSOID	70
WINDRAY	72
LAND OF FIRE	**74**
THE MANGKWAN CLAN	76
ASH VILLAGE	78
ASH VILLAGE LIFE	80
MANGKWAN WEAPONS	82
VARANG	84
VARANG'S YURT	86
NIGHTWRAITH	88
SWAMPLANDS	**90**
SWAMP LIFE	92
THE RDA	**94**
BRIDGEHEAD	96
RDA CONSTRUCTION BLIMP	98
SCI-OPS COMPLEX	100
SCANNER LAB	102
GENERAL ARDMORE	104
COLONEL MILES QUARITCH RECOM	106
CORPORAL LYLE WAINFLEET RECOM	108
PARKER SELFRIDGE	110
PERSONNEL EQUIPMENT	111
CAPTAIN MICK SCORESBY	112
DR. IAN GARVIN	113
ASH ENCAMPMENT	114
WILDLIFE CONTAINMENT UNIT	116
D-22 REMOTE-OPERATED BULLDOZER	118
MARITIME EXPANSION	120
FACTORY SHIP	122
HOLOTABLE	124
INDEX	126
ACKNOWLEDGMENTS	128

FOREWORD

Although it is almost two decades ago since I read the original screenplay of *Avatar*, I can still vividly recall my sense of astonishment and admiration at the exquisitely defined and articulated world of Pandora. The screenplay, almost a novel, positively burst with specifically detailed renderings, not only of character and place, but of beast and plant, vehicle and machine, weaponry, and wardrobe.

This remarkable assemblage of factual fiction was entirely the product of the mind, heart, soul, and imagination of James Cameron. Firing on all cylinders—as storyteller, filmmaker, engineer, scientist, artist, and spiritual seeker—Jim's comprehensive, indeed obsessive, attention and insistence on verisimilitude set a standard that has been emulated and observed throughout the expansive growth of the *Avatar* saga.

Cameron's imaginings continue to inspire and fuel an ever-expanding family of artists, designers, technicians, linguists, composers, and, of course, fans. This *Visual Dictionary* is a testament to both the individual and team efforts of so many creative minds at Lightstorm Entertainment and Wētā Workshop; their investment of time, energy, and passionate care is apparent on every page.

The old adage says that God is in the details. In this case, it can truly be said that *Eywa* is imbued and embedded in each word and illustration. Some nuggets are exotic, some highly technical, and some reveal aspects of the Na'vi that are almost, well, human. For example, the Tlalim clan, the peripatetic Wind Traders, are known throughout Pandora as not only the purveyors of news from afar, but also peddlers of gossip and tellers of tall tales.

This is but a single example of the myriad gems contained in this cornucopia of all things *Avatar*; an entertaining and valuable resource for Na'vi fan and Na'vi novice alike.

I began by recalling my astonishment and admiration for the original *Avatar* screenplay. Perhaps I remember it so clearly because I still feel it, and if, perhaps, a sense of wonder has become somewhat familiar, it is nevertheless still exhilarating and exciting. I expect that you will be thrilled and delighted as well.

And you will have questions because the more you learn, the more you will want to learn. Seeking and questioning. Such is the way of *Avatar*. There is more to come. Much more.

STEPHEN LANG
Colonel Miles Quaritch

PANDORA

SINCE ITS DISCOVERY in the Alpha Centauri system, Pandora has obsessed humankind. While Earth is dying due to the burden of billions of humans, the prospect of a new home in a rich and thriving biosphere gives many hope for the future. From space, the magnificent fifth moon of the gas giant Polyphemus resembles Earth in its prime: whorls of white cloud, green landmasses, and blue oceans. Though Pandora's atmosphere is deadly to humans, this new world exists in a state of grace. Its potential is limitless if harnessed correctly. As humans strengthen their foothold on the moon, development spreads, sparking hostility among the indigenous Na'vi over the growing threat to their native lands. Tensions flare in a battle for survival between cultures, with the fate of Pandora itself at stake.

THE OMATIKAYA

The Omatikaya are a friendly and deeply spiritual clan of Na'vi that reside in a rainforest. They were the first Na'vi to have contact with humans on Pandora. Also known as the "Blue Flute Clan," the clan are noted weavers recognized for their beautiful textiles and woven structures. They are also proud warriors and protectors of their home and way of life.

THE METKAYINA

The Metkayina are one of the sublittoral Na'vi cultures, known as "Reef People," that live along coastal reefs, barrier reefs, and atolls. Their tranquil island home is protected from the wild ocean by a natural seawall. Although Metkayina history is rife with conflict and hardships, the clan has learned to live peacefully and simply in harmony with their ocean biome.

THE TLALIM

The Tlalim, also known as the Wind Traders, are a nomadic clan that travels across Pandora by air. They sail the skies in convoys of woven gondolas held aloft by giant hydrogen-filled medusoids. While most Na'vi live by hunting and gathering, the Wind Traders are famous for bartering goods with other clans. They are great tellers of news, tall tales, and gossip.

EYWA

Eywa is the universal consciousness of Pandora and the balancing and guiding force behind its ecosytems. Considered a deity by the Na'vi, she works like a brain to ensure that the entire body of the moon is using its resources in as perfect a way as possible—a network that allows every species to live in harmony and balance with its environment. Trusting that *Eywa* will provide, all Na'vi practice The Three Laws:

- You shall not use the metals of the ground.
- You shall not carry burdens upon the turning wheel.
- You shall not set stone upon stone.

The Na'vi do not understand *Eywa*'s reasons for these three simple laws, but some believe that weapons of metal poison the heart and threaten to turn them into the very enemy they are fighting against.

THE MANGKWAN

The Mangkwan are Na'vi raiders, defined by the ash from the volcanic eruption that devastated—and continues to devastate—their home. Also known as the Ash People, they wear ash as a symbol of their rejection of *Eywa*, whom they blame for her lack of intervention during the decimation of their clan. They pillage neighboring villages, bringing death and destruction, and embrace a conqueror's path.

THE RDA

The Resources Development Administration (RDA) is a giant corporation with many subsidiaries that dominates all off-Earth mining and development throughout the Sol and Alpha Centauri systems. The RDA has monopoly rights to products shipped, derived, or developed from locations like Pandora. Subsidiaries include power utilities, manufacturing, defense, and pharmaceutical companies.

THE SULLY FAMILY

AGAINST THE BACKDROP of this "Time of Great Sorrow," the Sully family comes to terms with their own grief, having lost Neteyam, their eldest son, in the battle at Three Brothers Rocks. In their new home at the village of the Metkayina Reef People, Jake and Neytiri mourn in different ways, testing the bond between them. He channels his grief into preparing for an escalation of war against the RDA, while she turns to song and prayer. Their surviving children—Kiri, Lo'ak, and Tuktirey—struggle similarly, with anger, rebellion, and vulnerability. Despite everything, the Sullys remind themselves to stay strong. With their human friend Spider now living with them, the Sully kids cling to the hope that they will get through these hard times together.

JAKE SULLY

DATA FILE	
HUMAN NAME	Jacob "Jake" Sully
NA'VI NAME	Jake Sully
CLAN	Omatikaya originally, now Metkayina
CLAN POSITION	Hunter
BASE	High Camp and Metkayina Village

FOLLOWING THE LOSS of his oldest son Neteyam in the recent battle against the RDA, Jake defaults to warrior mode—a determined fighter and strategist. He dives down to the enemy's sunken SeaDragon to scavenge for assault rifles, ammo, and RPGs. Jake wants to arm the Na'vi with human weapons to enable them to fight on equal terms, but the People resist him, saying this is not "the Na'vi Way." They wish him to ride *toruk*, the great leonopteryx, and become the legendary hero *Toruk Makto* once again.

BEADED ARMBAND
Trinket is a seed from the Na'ring rainforest, adorned with elements from the reef

FLIGHT GEAR
When airborne, an *ikran* rider wears a visor to protect their eyes from the force of the wind.

Braided leather

JAKE'S *IKRAN*-RIDING VISOR

AR holster attaches to ikran saddle

JAKE'S ASSAULT RIFLE AND HOLSTER

THE OUTRIDER

When it is clear that Spider cannot live in a breathing mask day and night at the reef, Jake takes him back to High Camp, the enclave of human loyalists, for his safety. Jake requests transport for his family with the Wind Traders. He offers himself and Neytiri to fly as outriders and guard the flotilla. This proposal is initially met with hesitation by the fleet's captain, Peylak, given Jake and Neytiri's profile as the top enemies of the RDA. Peylak relents in view of the rising aggression of the Mangkwan—the Ash People—who have been known to prey upon the Wind Traders' airborne caravans.

Jake guards the Wind Trader flotilla as an outrider.

knife with woven grip

THE SULLY FAMILY

FACT FILE
> Jake resumes his guerilla raids against the RDA on the mainland to disrupt its expansion and mislead Quaritch's search parties. It also serves as an outlet for the toll both have taken on his marriage.

- Button from Grace's lab coat
- A lock of Kiri's hair
- Crafted from spade wing spine
- Gifted by Neytiri; bead symbolizes their meeting

JAKE'S KNIFE

JAKE'S KNIFE SHEATH

JAKE'S SONGCORD

MAINTAINING THE EDGE
Jake continually resharpens Na'vi weapons for survival and protection

- Comms earpiece
- Metkayina chest guard

MASTERING THE BEAST
Tonowari, *olo'eyktan* of the Metkayina clan, tells Jake that only *Toruk Makto* can unite the clans into a force mighty enough to defeat the RDA. Jake fears invoking *toruk*, because his previous union with Pandora's apex aerial predator unleashed a raging beast within himself. Many of the Na'vi who followed him into battle died as a result and he has carried the guilt for 15 long years. However, Tonowari convinces Jake that, in these desperate times, he must unleash the Beast of War once more. Jake can only hope that his experience as a father and leader will temper his inner demons. He returns to the mountains to reunite with the legendary beast and become *Toruk Makto*, "Rider of Last Shadow."

TORUK

HERO OF THE NA'VI
Bowing to his destiny, Jake once again flies with *toruk* as the mythic leader *Toruk Makto*, casting his great shadow over many clans, and uniting them into a single formidable fighting force.

13

NEYTIRI

EVERY DAY, during the daily eclipse, Neytiri mourns the traditional way for her son Neteyam, singing his life as recorded in the beads of his songcord. She is in a place of darkness and solitude, without her home, her People, even her father's bow, which lies broken at the bottom of the ocean following the battle with the RDA at the Three Brothers Rocks. She has only a single flame of hope: her faith that this is all part of *Eywa*'s plan. Neytiri is a believer in the Great Mother preserving the balance of all life.

Neytiri wears Neteyam's necklace while grieving

NETEYAM'S NECKLACE

THANATOR TOP
Neytiri's thanator (*palulukan*) top honors the power of the apex land predator, which Neytiri was the first Na'vi to ever ride as a mount in the Battle of Hallelujah Mountains.

INTERNAL CONFLICT
All that Neytiri believes to be good is threatened by humans. She hates their insatiable aggression and resents the blood of their race in her husband and children. Filled with anger and wishing for revenge for everything taken from her, she will do whatever it takes to rid Pandora of this human plague. These feelings are an unspoken source of conflict between herself and Jake. She makes him feel that his choices as a human led to the death of Neteyam, their eldest son, the Golden Boy of the family. She also resents the present situation— being away from her forest clan and staying out of the war in order to protect Spider. Neytiri and Jake must resolve their differences to win the war against the RDA and save the People.

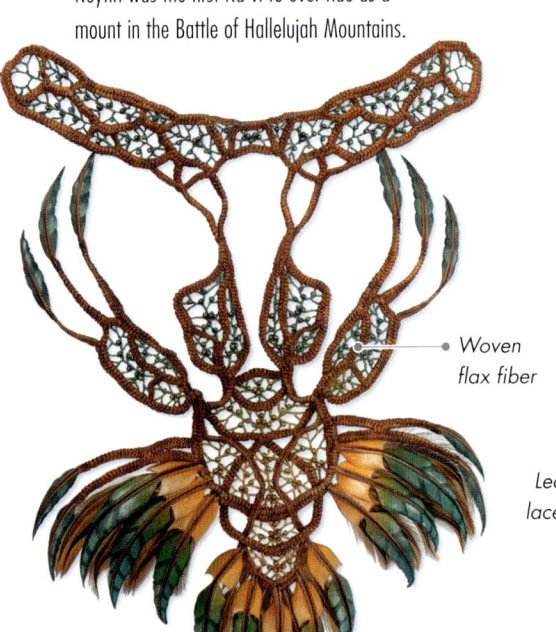

Woven flax fiber

Leather thonging laced over sheath

Gold fronds; a Metkayina fringe-style loincloth

NEYTIRI'S KNIFE AND SHEATH

Made wholly from natural plant materials, including warbonnet seeds

ARMBAND

FACT FILE
> Passionate, caring, and loyal, Neytiri is determined to perform her duty as mother and *tsakarem* and to protect her family.

DATA FILE
FULL NA'VI NAME *Neytiri te Tskaha Mo'atite*

CLAN Omatikaya

CLAN POSITION *Tsakarem* (*tsahik*-in-waiting)

BASE OF OPERATIONS High Camp and Metkayina Village

THE SULLY FAMILY

STRONG HEART

The warrior blood of her ancestors runs strong in Neytiri. She serves as protector to the Na'vi and her family. When she notices the same strength flowing through her son, Lo'ak, she is torn between keeping him safe and letting his destiny play out. As a child, she met the power of the forest on her own and returned stronger from it. Now she is ready with her fighting and riding skills, confident in the spirit of her People, who have faced and overcome adversity since time immemorial. As both a mighty warrior and a mother, Neytiri resolves to fight alongside Jake with the clans, setting an inspiring example for her children to follow.

- Birth of Lo'ak; a drop of his blood encased in amber
- Adoption of Kiri; a drop of her blood encased in amber
- Birth of Tuktirey; a drop of blood encased in amber
- Birth of Neteyam; a drop of his blood encased in amber
- Grace's death; a bead from Grace's necklace
- Joining the Metkayina clan; a piece of reef shell
- Jake enters her life

NEYTIRI'S SONGCORD

- Layered with tough fish scales

ARMGUARD

- red braided wrap
- Each long, blue vane is a single piece held in place by the red braided wrap. They cross each other inside the bow

NEYTIRI'S BROKEN WAR BOW
Broken from the battle at Three Brothers Rocks, Neytiri's war bow was on the SeaDragon when it sank to the bottom of the ocean.

- War paint inspired by the colors of Neytiri's first ikran, Seze, represents her warrior spirit
- Jake's handprint signifies their bond and unified strong hearts

Neytiri still wears traditional mourning paint weeks after Neteyam's death.

15

KIRI

WHENEVER HER ADOPTIVE FAMILY connects to the Spirit Tree at the Cove of the Ancestors, Kiri wishes she could join them, but has been told by Dr. Norm Spellman that another underwater seizure would be fatal. Different from other Na'vi, she is confused by her innate power to influence nature and the presence of *Eywa*, who feels so close that Kiri believes she can hear *Eywa*'s heart beating. Kiri is drawn to the Spirit Tree as a portal to the *Oma* (the Spirit World) and for a possible connection to their deity, *Eywa*, the Great Mother. By linking to it, she hopes to learn more about why she is the way she is, and hopefully who her biological father is, a mystery that has never been resolved. When Jake and Neytiri decide to take Spider back to High Camp, she jumps at the chance to go with them, to try connecting to the terrestrial Tree of Souls, which may be safer for her.

VINE TOP

This chest adornment makes Kiri feel close to the Na'ring rainforest she first called home.

- Bioluminescent dots can flare up during deep, emotionally charged moments, a rare trait in Na'vi
- Beaded ladder top
- Medicine pouch

SELF DEFENSE
Though not a warrior like Jake and Neytiri, Kiri has been trained to use her knife for protection.

KNIFE AND SHEATH

BEADED BELT

SEEKING ANSWERS

Kiri believes she has been put on Pandora for a reason but is unsure what that is. Her biological mother, Grace Augustine, exists only through recordings (and also in *Eywa*) and her father is unknown, leaving no one to answer her questions. But she has the support of her adoptive family—Jake, Neytiri, her siblings—and her friends, especially Spider. At times, she and Spider live in their own world, exploring the forest, and later the ocean, together. Although directly contacting *Eywa* has up to now proved not only fruitless but extremely dangerous, Spider's presence gives Kiri the confidence to define and understand herself.

Metkayina armband adorned with abalone shell chips

FACT FILE

> Kiri's uncanny connectivity to all flora and fauna gives her a natural empathy for all hurt, wounded, and isolated beings.

THE SULLY FAMILY

Kiri may at times seem aloof or distant, but she is merely absorbing the larger world around her with all her senses, while also trying to understand how she fits in it.

Often reflects on good memories with Neteyam

KIRI'S SONGCORD

TRUE TO HERSELF

Some of the clan Na'vi feel that Kiri not only behaves strangely but has done things that can't be explained, even by the two *tsahik* (shamans) Ronal and Mo'at. Ronal especially grows afraid of her power, and some of the reef kids treat her as a freak. Kiri hates feeling different from the other kids. Her power also takes a physical toll on her, as when, in the rainforest, she wills mycelium from the ground to colonize Spider's body and enable him to breathe the Pandoran air, saving his life. But if using her abilities to help others puts her at risk, she wouldn't want it any other way.

ABALONE WRIST CUFF

Kiri's most sacred piece, still kept intact

GRACE'S NECKLACE

HAIR BEADS

Beads crafted from panopyra, helicoradian, and scorpion thistle seeds from the rainforest.

PANDORAN LEAVES

Like most Na'vi, Kiri uses feather-like leaf-scales as the base material for ornamentation and structural components

BEADED ARMBAND

Crafted with material Kiri gathered during her return to High Camp

DATA FILE	
NA'VI NAME	Kiri te Suli Kireysi'ite
CLAN	Omatikaya
CLAN POSITION	Tsakarem
BASE	High Camp and Metkayina Village

17

LO'AK

BEING A NA'VI brings expectations that challenge Lo'ak as the mixed-race son of a Na'vi mother and a human-Na'vi hybrid father. Though it is never said, he senses that the clans think he's not as strong as other Na'vi because of the human element of his lineage—evident in his four-fingered hands (true-born Na'vi only have three fingers and a thumb on each hand). Lo'ak's self-esteem sinks even lower after his brother's death, for which he blames himself. Jake, who always pushed his son to measure up, has become even more demanding, which Lo'ak interprets as unspoken blame for Neteyam's death. Though he doesn't realize it, however, Lo'ak is a natural leader, more like his father than even Jake realizes.

DATA FILE
NA'VI NAME Lo'ak te Suli Tsyeyk'itan
CLAN Omatikaya and Metkayina
CLAN POSITION Warrior in training
BASE High Camp and Metkayina Village

IKRAN RIDING VISOR

NETEYAM'S BEADED CHOKER
Lo'ak wears Neteyam's choker to honor his brother's memory.

FATHER AND SON
Lo'ak has a tense relationship with his father, who is overly judgmental whenever Lo'ak makes a mistake. Neytiri realizes how difficult it must be for her youngest son to grow up in the shadow of the great *Toruk Makto*, especially as a mixed-race kid. It's not that Jake doesn't love Lo'ak—he loves him deeply, understanding what it's like to lose a brother and be vulnerable as well as rebellious. But Jake knows that in a time of war he must toughen his son and make him as strong as possible. Jake must also learn to trust Lo'ak to forge his own path and uncover his hidden strengths.

Shells collected and gifted by Tuktirey

ARMBAND

Leather from an ax head Pandoran shark

LO'AK'S METKAYINA KNIFE AND SHEATH

HONED BLADE
Lo'ak's first tool and weapon was a knife, and through experience, each iteration has been more precisely suited to him.

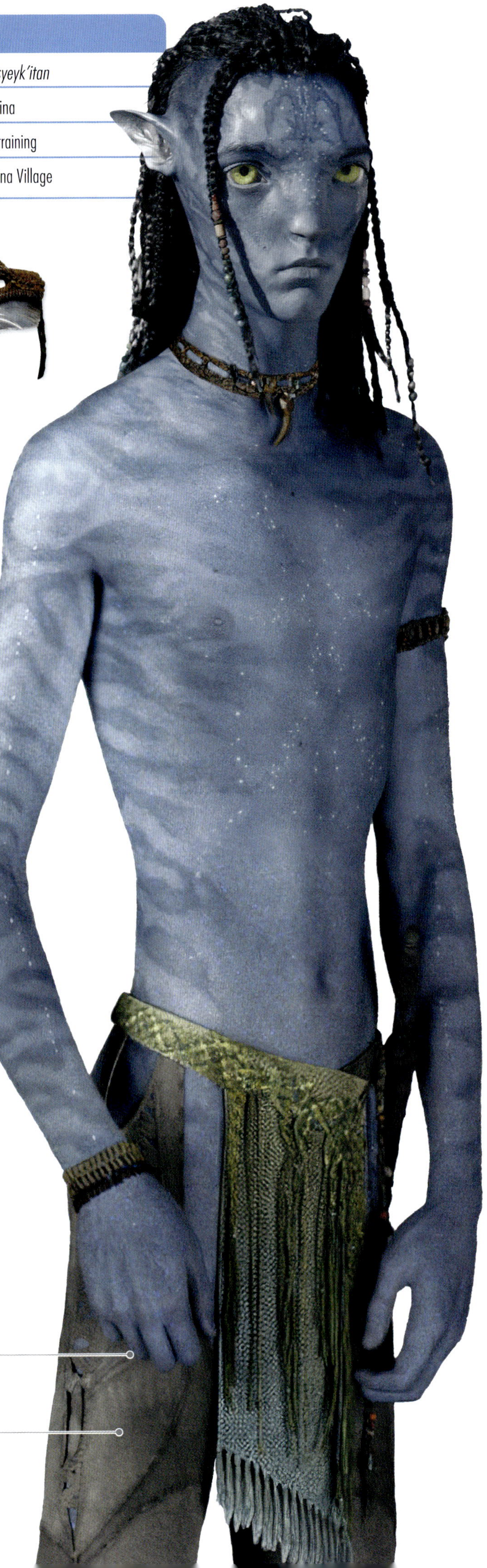

Four-fingered hands

Omatikaya breeches

THE SULLY FAMILY

FACT FILE

> Lo'ak is determined to prove to his family that's he's not a failure, nor is he "second best."
> Lo'ak finds strength in being able to speak openly with his family and friends, knowing he'll be heard, even when it's hard.

A LOYAL FRIEND

The *tulkun* Payakan is an outcast and Lo'ak, who also feels rejected, is drawn to his plight. Lo'ak goes through the bonding ceremony with Payakan, becoming Brother of Tulkun. However, the Reef Clan, reprimand him for bonding with Payakan. Lo'ak stands up for his friend, not only defending him from the RDA, but also the Reef Na'vi. After the battle at Three Brothers Rocks, Lo'ak's friends agree that Payakan is a hero, but they also respect The Tulkun Way. Killing only leads to more killing, and Payakan is held responsible for the deaths of the *tulkun* and Na'vi he led into battle. However, Lo'ak will not deny the bond he shares with Payakan and will remain at his side regardless of any social consequences.

BRACELET
- Leather base

RESTORED
Lo'ak and Tsireya repair Neytiri's war bow through shaving, lamination, shaping, and fine smoothing for shine, finishing with carved detailing.
- Draw knife for shaving

LO'AK'S SONGCORD
- Bead in memory of his first ikran
- Rock for sanding
- Rocks for polishing
- Scriber for carving

NEYTIRI'S MENDED WAR BOW
- Weaving details of the bow were done by Tsireya

- Chest guard symbolizes that Lo'ak has come of age and can act as a warrior for the Metkayina

Lo'ak and Tsireya recover Neytiri's broken war bow from the SeaDragon wreck.

TUKTIREY

WHENEVER SHE'S FEELING SCARED, Tuk is reassured by her father and mother, trusting that their family can overcome anything together. She never wants to be apart from her siblings, no matter what they're doing. In a pinch, she is tough and resilient and can be counted upon to help. She is innately empathetic, especially with Kiri and Spider, both of whom she loves. Eventually her siblings don't see Tuk as a tag-along anymore, but as an integral part of the team.

SONGCORD

Represents High Camp, where she can see above Pandora

Tuk's first armband she wove by herself

PINK SHELL ARMBAND

SHELL BRACELETS

KNIFE
Though smaller than adult knives, a child's knife can be used for cooking, cutting, and protection against modest-sized animals.

Metkayina style of weaving taught by Tsireya

MULTICULTURAL CHILD

Tuk is too young to complete Omatikaya rites of passage such as a first hunt or bonding with an *ikran*. However, she is familiar with these rituals through play, practicing with a child's bow and arrow or a sticky *ikran* catcher. Now living with the Metkayina, Tuk is exposed to new customs on the reef. While her parents continue to teach her the traditions of their ancestral home, they also help her to adjust to life on the island, maintaining the values and continuity of both cultures. This allows Tuk to appreciate her unique identity as she grows up in an increasingly complex world.

Rows of small purple beads made by the same technique that Neytiri used for her wrist cuff

DATA FILE	
FULL NA'VI NAME	Tuktirey te Suli Neytiri'ite
CLAN	Omatikaya
BASE	High Camp and Metkayina Village

THE SULLY FAMILY

Tuk runs through the reef village with Spider, excited to see her father and brother returning home after a day of ocean scavenging.

FACT FILE
> Tuk wants to join any adventure her older siblings are involved in.
> She is always in the thick of things and refuses to be left behind.

Anklet

SHELL ARMBAND

WIND TRADER CHILD'S CLOAK

KNIFE SHEATH
Tuk retrieves her Omatikaya knife sheath at High Camp, confident it is rugged enough to withstand reef conditions.

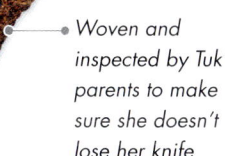

• Woven and inspected by Tuk's parents to make sure she doesn't lose her knife

LEAF *KURU* ADORNMENTS

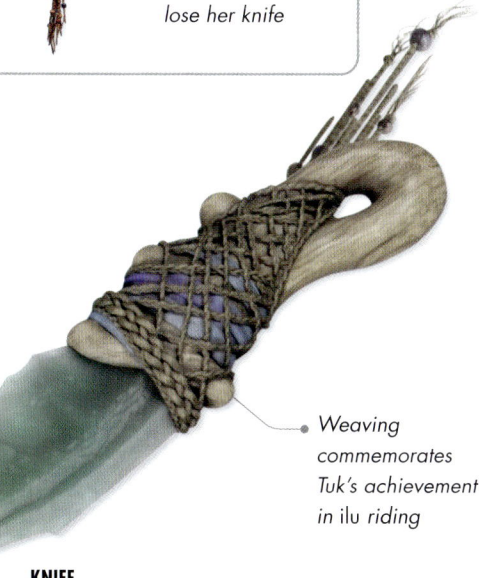

• Weaving commemorates Tuk's achievement in ilu riding

KNIFE

PUSHING FORWARD
The Sully family takes strength from Tuk's fierce spirit just as much as she does from theirs. Surviving several dangerous situations, she is still able to find joy living in the moment, whether dancing with Wind Traders or riding an *ilu*. The wonder in her laughter resonates in her family's hearts, raising their morale. They tell Tuk that Sullys never quit, reminding her how strong they are and of her own ability to prevail over any obstacle.

THE OMATIKAYA CLAN & ALLIES

OF ALL NA'VI CLANS on Pandora, the Omatikaya understand the threat of the RDA best, as they have lost the most, including their beloved *Kelutral*, their ancestral Hometree. They've also done the most to protect their homeland. Under Jake's leadership, the clan has attacked RDA maglev trains, mining operations, and pipelines around Bridgehead in fierce guerrilla operations, seizing weapons and hitting the RDA where it hurts—their pocketbook. Jake's main aim is to wear down the corporation until it loses the economic ability to continue colonization. When he must evacuate his family to safety, Jake hands the reins of leadership to Tarsem, who becomes the new *olo'eyktan*. Tarsem leads the Omatikaya in the fight for their territory against the encroaching RDA development. He is hopeful that one day the clan will return to its peaceful way of life, but for now he and the

OMATIKAYA LIFE

AS THE FIGHT for their land continues, the Omatikaya keep a light footprint in the rainforest. By the grace of *Eywa*'s immune response against the RDA, they are able to visit sacred sites for rituals, as well as hunt and gather just enough to meet their bare minimum needs, without disturbance. The clan has always been generous with its resources, but in wartime, that instinct becomes more pronounced: everyone looks out for one another, helping with food, clothing, and maintaining morale through shared music, storytelling, and dance. In times of great struggle, the People come together.

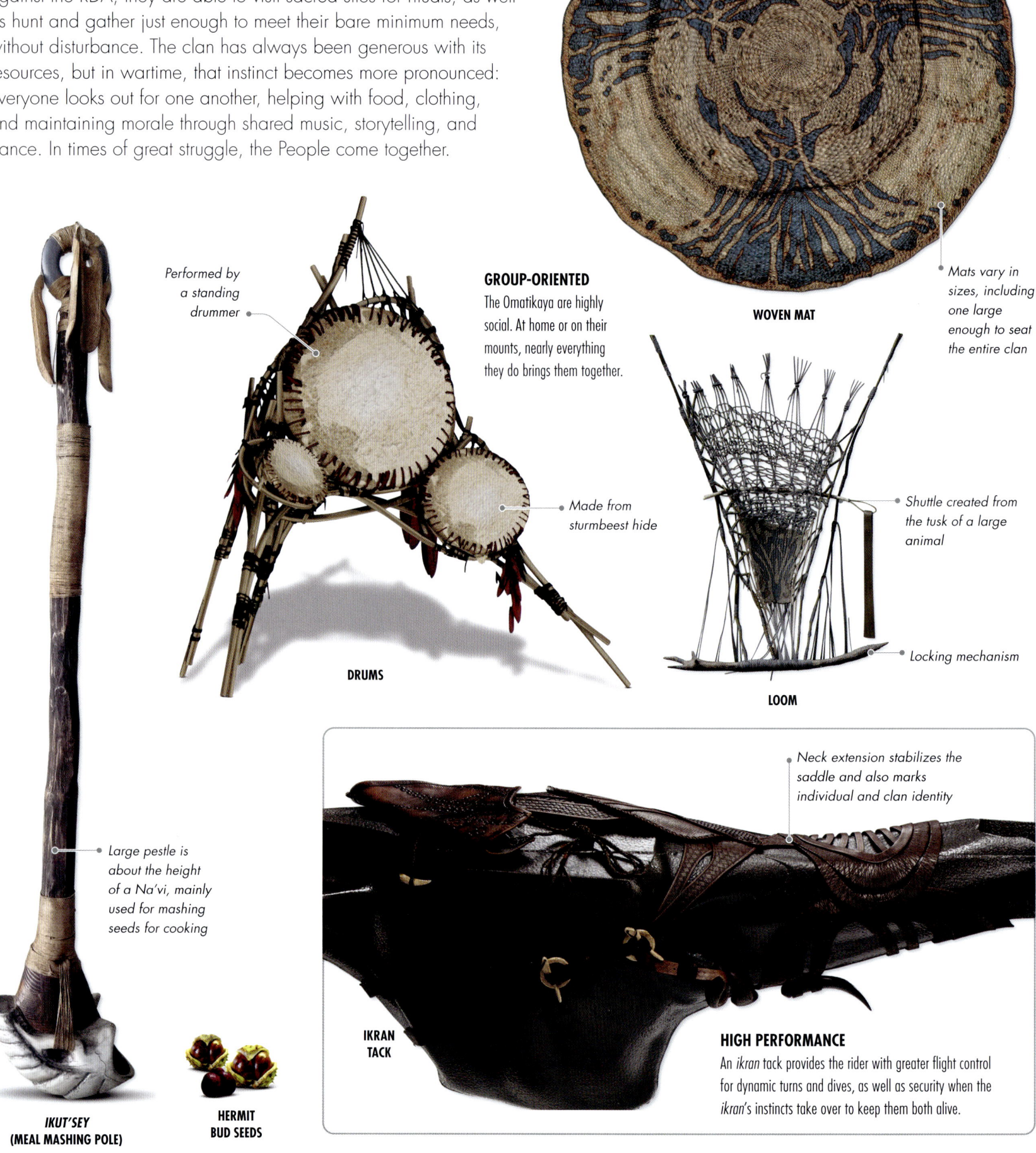

WOVEN MAT

Mats vary in sizes, including one large enough to seat the entire clan

Performed by a standing drummer

GROUP-ORIENTED
The Omatikaya are highly social. At home or on their mounts, nearly everything they do brings them together.

Made from sturmbeest hide

DRUMS

Shuttle created from the tusk of a large animal

Locking mechanism

LOOM

Large pestle is about the height of a Na'vi, mainly used for mashing seeds for cooking

IKUT'SEY
(MEAL MASHING POLE)

HERMIT BUD SEEDS

IKRAN TACK

Neck extension stabilizes the saddle and also marks individual and clan identity

HIGH PERFORMANCE
An *ikran* tack provides the rider with greater flight control for dynamic turns and dives, as well as security when the *ikran*'s instincts take over to keep them both alive.

OMATIKAYA TOYS

THE OMATIKAYA CLAN & ALLIES

NEW TOYS are harder to come by, as the Omatikaya manage their resources more carefully. But the children don't seem to mind. Omatikaya toys are built to last, letting kids imagine and explore freely. Parents watch with delight as their children build upon older toys, adding beading, carvings, and scavenged parts. Through play, Na'vi children develop creativity and problem-solving skills, learn cooperation and value, and give parents the chance to see what to encourage or correct. It's no easy task, as any Omatikaya parent will admit, but it is rewarding when they see their children grow, reconcile faults, and begin to contribute to the community.

CULTURAL HERITAGE
Toys help children connect with clan history, instilling a sense of heritage and belonging.

HANDS ON
Kinetic toys help Na'vi children to explore how things work and see the world in new ways.

- Blue thread for crest
- **TORUK TOY**
- Beading added to passed-down item
- The flexible wood spiral opens and closes as the cord pulls, making rattling clatter
- Tassels that children love to see move
- Hand-sized wooden figure carved with a single knife, often gifted to children
- **WHIRLIGIG**
- Carved from fallen mangrove root
- **DIREHORSE TOY**

TUK'S *TULKUN* TOY

After Tuk arrives at the reef, she is introduced to the *tulkun*. She's heard of the intelligent ocean species but has never seen one. By crafting her own wooden totem of the *tulkun*, she creates an opportunity to ask questions about all aspects of the species and understand them better, allowing her to integrate them into her life and learn new things.

25

MO'AT

TSAHÌK OF THE OMATIKAYA, Mo'at's role is to minister to her clan's physical and spiritual health, and also interpret the will of *Eywa* through signs and manifestations. For this she draws upon thousands of years of shamanic practice, including ritual and the mastery of forest plant extracts and herbs. Mo'at has experienced profound personal loss over the course of her storied history and, following Neteyam's passing, now provides the guidance the Sully family needs to heal and move forward.

FACT FILE

> Mo'at places her trust in Jake, who was brought to her People by *Eywa*, when he arms them with weapons of metal.

> In response to the Sky People's weapons, Mo'at has decided that her clan should perform a spiritual cleansing ritual to purge themselves of their influence after each use.

RITUAL STAFF
Mo'at draws upon millennia of shamanic practice, where the *tsahìk*'s staff is carried in ceremony.

The tsahìk Sees into the staff, a metaphor for the one who interprets the will of Eywa through signs and manifestations. The Omatikaya Hometree can be observed encased in the amber

- Bead symbolizes her bond with Eytukan
- Woodsprite-shaped seed represents her role as tsahìk

MO'AT'S SONGCORD

- Wood and amber staff
- Woven choker
- Inspired by the tree root system that links to Eywa

TSAHÌK TOP

- Amber headband
- Tsahìk's needle-casing ornamentation
- Braided kuru
- Long beaded loincloth

THE BELIEVER
Mo'at is able to communicate with and translate the will of *Eywa*. In her infinite wisdom, she is certain Kiri has been given an ability that cannot be explained in any way but by the deity. During these trying times, Mo'at has faith that *Eywa* has a greater plan to see the Na'vi through.

DATA FILE

NA'VI NAME	*Mo'at te Pohatsua Oma'ite*
CLAN	Omatikaya
CLAN POSITION	*Tsahik*, clan matriarch
BASE	High Camp

TARSEM

A DISTINGUISHED HUNTER and warrior, Tarsem is wise for his years. He is the new *olo'eyktan* of the Omatikaya clan, after Jake Sully. Focused and compassionate, he is open to new ways of thinking. Like all great leaders before him, Tarsem is dedicated to the survival of the People in times of conflict. Often, he will be seen flying at the helm of an aerial campaign or a search and rescue operation. His clan respects him for his courage and compassion.

DATA FILE
NA'VI NAME Tarsem te Kumon Arun'itan
CLAN Omatikaya
CLAN POSITION Olo'eyktan
BASE High Camp

HAIR ADORNMENT

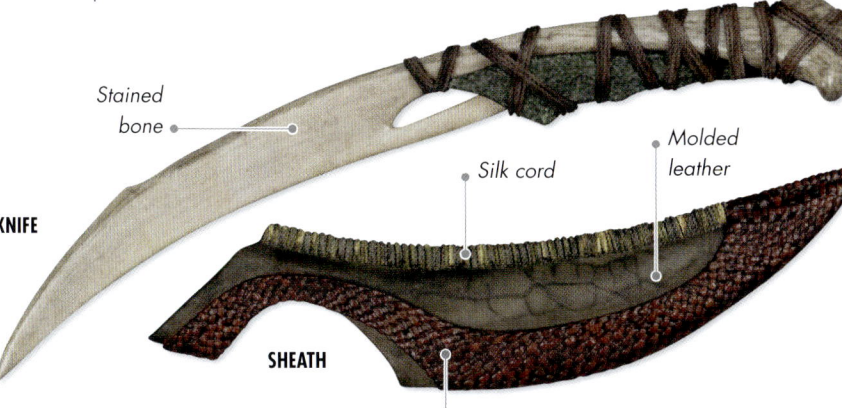

KNIFE — Stained bone
SHEATH — Silk cord, Molded leather, Braided leather

THE VANGUARD
After receiving Mo'at's blessing, Tarsem became one of the first Na'vi to follow Jake and take up weapons of metal.

OLO'EYKTAN CUMMERBUND

- Patterns and beads are a storied history for each Omatikaya *olo'eyktan* and *olo'eykte*
- The clan heirloom has been re-leathered over generations

Armguard made from plant fibers

Colors inspired by his friend and mentor, Akwey

ARMBAND

FACT FILE
> Tarsem's patience with others inspires them to have faith in themselves.
> Fully aware of the Sky People's motivations, Tarsem understands the responsibilities he bears to protect his People.

Leg guards for flying ikran

Tarsem leads members of the Omatikaya mounted on *ikran*.

DR. NORM SPELLMAN

SURPRISINGLY ADAPTABLE, Norm moves through the human and Na'vi worlds easily, functioning in avatar form out in the wilds of Pandora or as a human at the biolab. He faithfully continues Grace Augustine's work and leads scientific exploration of their exo-moon world. Though not a warrior at heart, he will rise to the occasion when necessary to defend the Na'vi People. He can handle weapons and respond to a crisis. When Neytiri lands at High Camp with an arrow through her lung, he performs emergency surgery, applying human medical techniques that the Na'vi don't traditionally practice. Norm acknowledges the power of Na'vi shamanic medicine, but he and Mo'at both know there are times when only "Sky People" medicine can save a life. Mo'at has confidence in Norm when human medical intervention is required, while Norm is eager to continue learning the secrets of Na'vi plant medicine from Mo'at. Norm stands as a leader and role model for the human Resistance living with the Omatikaya and acts as a diplomat to the Na'vi.

- Norm has learned to function with minimal sleep
- AR with personalized weaving
- First-aid kit

TRUSTED FRIEND

Norm is astonished when he learns that Spider can breathe the Pandoran air without a mask, accepting that there is still a lot to learn about the moon's biology compared to Earth's. More importantly, he is relieved Spider is still alive and perfectly healthy. After all, Norm's main focus is to ensure the well-being of everyone he cares about and their environment. He listens to Jake's concern about the mycelium growing inside and sustaining Spider—that it could enable the RDA's eventual conquest of Pandora. As Jake's confidant and companion, Norm supports Jake's strategies and whatever decisions he makes to protect the People and Pandora. But he also knows his role is to warn Jake, and play devil's advocate when necessary.

DATA FILE	
NAME	Dr. Norm Spellman
AFFILIATION	Omatikaya
PROFESSION	Xenoanthropologist
BASE	High Camp

Sturmbeest hide sheath

KNIFE AND SHEATH

Norm observes a scan of the mycelium growing inside Spider.

THE OMATIKAYA CLAN & ALLIES

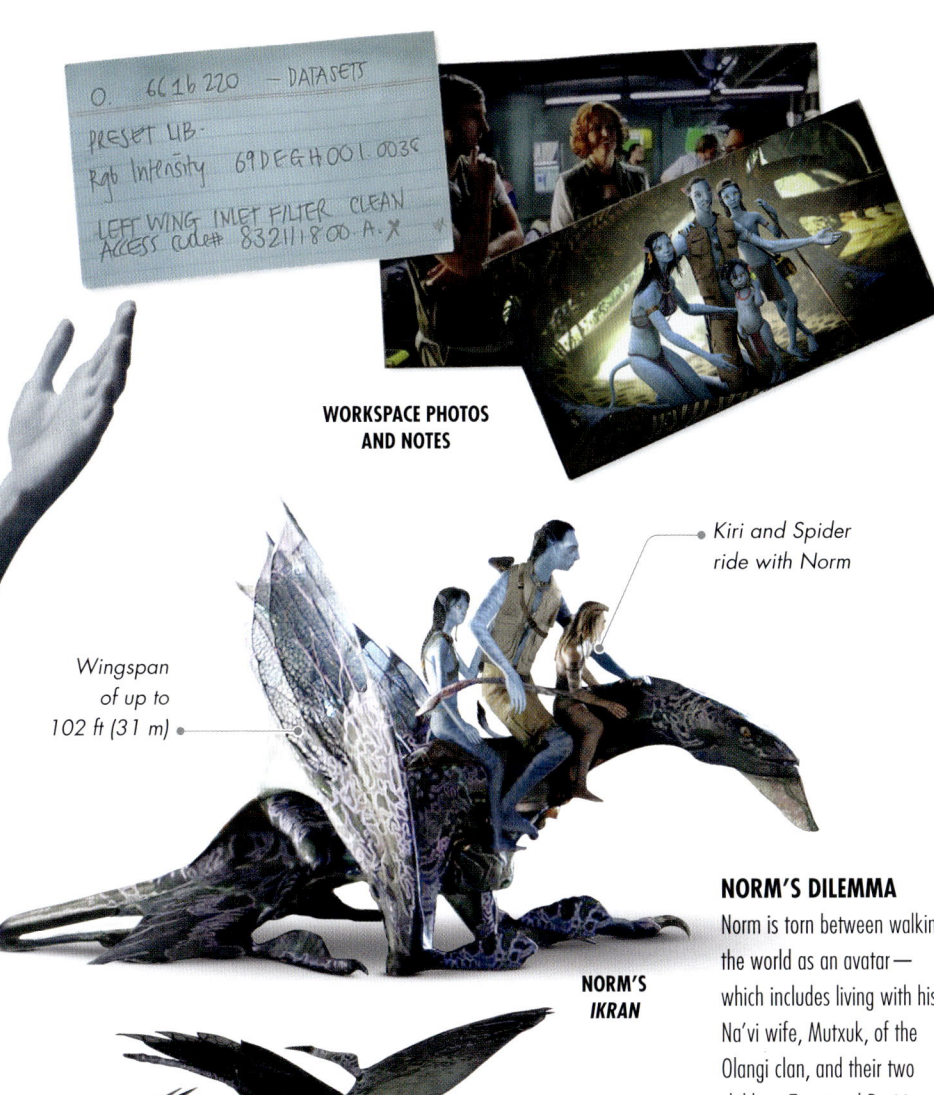

WORKSPACE PHOTOS AND NOTES

FACT FILE

> Norm has written many scientific papers on Na'vi culture and medicine, but has never been able to have them peer reviewed or published, because he is cut off from the human mainstream in his role as a guerrilla fighter loyal to Jake.
> Norm has overcome his trauma from the Battle of the Hallelujah Mountains to be able to continue the fight against the RDA alongside Jake.
> Torn between two worlds, Norm needs to feel alive as a human just as he does as an avatar, a delicate balance that only a small number of individuals truly understand.

Kiri and Spider ride with Norm

Wingspan of up to 102 ft (31 m)

NORM'S IKRAN

NORM'S DILEMMA
Norm is torn between walking the world as an avatar—which includes living with his Na'vi wife, Mutxuk, of the Olangi clan, and their two children, Tuvat and Popiti—and living in his human body.

BANDOLIER

Fine Omatikayan weaving

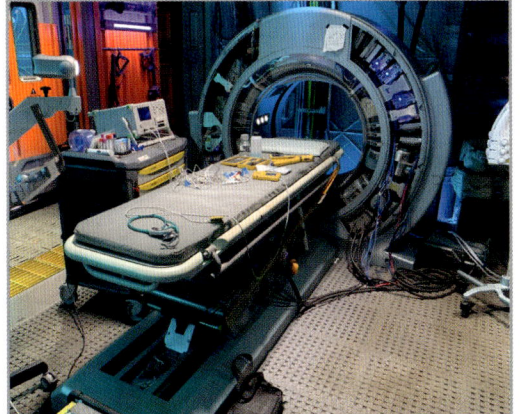

OLD TECHNOLOGY
The decades-old link unit requires constant upkeep, but remains a workhorse. In addition to linking drivers to their avatars, it also provides medical readouts.

DR. MAX PATEL

THE HARD-WORKING CHIEF SCIENTIST of the Avatar Program, Dr. Max Patel is dedicated to the welfare of others. When he learns of Spider's air-breathing transformation, he commits himself fully to the boy's well-being and to solving the mystery of what's going on inside him biologically. Monitoring Kiri's seizure condition has already involved him more deeply in the Sullys' lives; ensuring Spider's health increases his importance to the future of Pandora. Fortunately, he has Norm and a reliable team of avatar scientists for support.

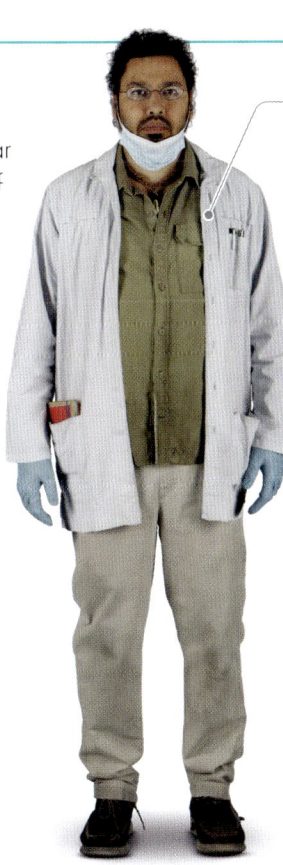

Lab coat

FACT FILE

> Despite current conditions on Pandora, Max ensures a safe and cheerful environment for the Sully kids at the biolab.

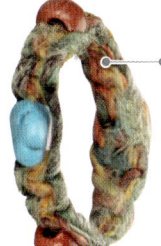

Max is married to Nora, a grower in charge of the food farms at High Camp.

DATA FILE

NAME	Dr. Max Patel
AFFILIATION	Omatikaya
PROFESSION	Chief Scientist of the Avatar Program
BASE	High Camp

Max aids Spider in adapting to life as a Pandoran air breather.

SPIDER

BORN ON AN ALIEN WORLD, Miles "Spider" Socorro is a true Pandoran. Although looked after by humans when growing up as an orphan at the Hell's Gate base, he spent most of his time on adventures with the Sully kids. He grew up in the Na'vi Way of thinking, believing in the balance of nature and the interconnectedness of all life. Spider longs to be accepted by the Omatikaya and live as much as a Na'vi as possible. He would love nothing more than to be adopted by Jake and Neytiri, like Kiri was, and truly join the Sully family. But though Neytiri tolerates him as a friend to their kids, he is the son of their greatest enemy, Colonel Miles Quaritch, and she will never accept him as a Sully. His strong moral code drove him to rescue his father's Recombinant from a watery grave after Jake left him for dead deep inside the SeaDragon wreck. Now living with the Sullys on the reef and aware that their adversary is still out there, Spider lives with a secret he can never reveal, even to Kiri, his closest friend.

TRUE COMPANIONS

The Sully kids have known Spider ever since he swapped his diapers for a loincloth. Though Neytiri frowns at her kids for hanging out with him, they are drawn to him for his sense of fun and loyalty. Spider understands Neytiri's suffering and ironically shares her hatred of the invaders, even though he is the same species. However, he hopes that one day she will see what her children see and accept him, too. Of the Sully kids, Spider has a particularly close bond with Kiri, who is also viewed by the clan as different. Together, they wonder about their place in the natural order of things. They explore Pandora as constant companions, a quest of self-discovery for both of them.

- Breathing mask connected to breather unit
- Omatikayan armband
- Exo-pack breather unit

- Carved wood, with lenses fashioned from chandelier fish membranes

SWIMMING GOGGLES

- Seeds from a grub plant

ANKLET

Kiri causes mycelium to grow from the forest floor, saving Spider's life; Lo'ak and Tuk look on in amazement.

THE OMATIKAYA CLAN & ALLIES

DATA FILE

NAME Miles "Spider" Socorro

AGE 16

AFFILIATION Omatikaya

BASE High Camp

KNIFE AND SHEATH
- Hide from a hunting trip organized by the Metkayina
- Palm fibers, gathered only after Spider had given a Na'vi thank-you blessing to the tree

- Learning to hunt with Lo'ak and Neteyam

GROWTH SPURT

When Spider is dying of asphyxiation in the forest, Kiri goes into a trance, calling upon her deeply buried powers. She places the seed-pod of a woodsprite into his mouth and, in order to save his life, commands the roots of the forest to cover him in mycelium, a silk-like cocoon. The same mycelium that forms the rainforest's neural network, plunges deep beneath Spider's skin and colonizes his anatomy, altering his blood chemistry, nervous system, and lungs at a cellular level. He emerges from this transformation able to breathe Pandoran air without an exo-pack. The changes are so significant on an epigenetic level that he begins to grow a *kuru* at the base of his skull.

NECKLACE

- Demand regulator bottle

EXO-PACK BREATHER UNIT

ARMBAND

- Made of abalone to show his appreciation for Metkayina village

- Bead celebrating Kiri's completion of Iknimaya, Na'vi rites of passage, with the Sully family

AIR SUPPLY
Breather units depend on battery replacements or alternative power sources, which limits being in the field for extended periods of time.

FACT FILE

> Like any frontier kid, growing up on Pandora seems the most natural thing in the world to Spider. He knows its dangers but still calls it home.

> Spider is proud to know more Na'vi dance moves than any other avatar and human.

> Spider speaks fluent Na'vi and has a good knowledge of Omatikaya culture and the rainforest; capable at archery and Na'vi hunting skills.

OMA EXPLORER
Spider becomes the first human being in history with the ability to bond with Pandoran creatures, and also connect to the global neural network, the *Oma*. Kiri becomes his coach in bonding with the animals of Pandora, and will act as his guide in the Spirit World among the ancestors. Once Spider connects to the *Oma*, his life experience and the essence of his being is uploaded into the global memory cloud so that, like all Na'vi, he can someday have immortality in the world-mind of *Eywa*.

SPIDER'S SONGCORD

NEVER ALONE

Spider knows his biological father is dead, and only a Recombinant based on his genome and imprinted with his memories now exists. The fact that Recom Quaritch grows fond of him causes them both to wonder whether there may still be a true family connection, albeit an unusual one. This leaves Spider emotionally confused. As an orphan, he is desperate for family; on the other hand, he knows Quaritch is the mortal enemy of the only family he has ever known, the Sullys. Spider is beginning to understand that the world is not black and white, and he must learn to live in the gray area. Fortunately, he is not alone. Along with Kiri, he is surrounded with solid role models like Jake, Norm, and the Avatar Program scientists.

IKEYNI

OLO'EYKTE OF THE TAYRANGI CLAN of the Eastern Sea, Ikeyni is one of the most tactically aware Na'vi leaders on Pandora. She is a superb *ikran* rider and warrior. Her archery skills while flying are unmatched, except by Neytiri. Ikeyni's thinking is always one or two steps ahead of her contemporaries, which Jake Sully recognizes. He knows she is one of his strongest allies.

Blade fashioned from the tooth of a nalutsa bull

KNIFE

Rusty red war paint rallies the Tayrangi to battle

Armguard made from turtapede hide, naturally adapted to saltwater ocean

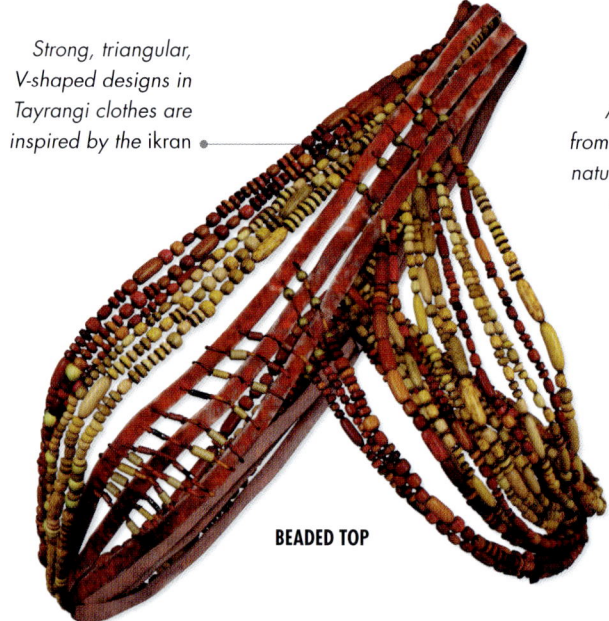

Strong, triangular, V-shaped designs in Tayrangi clothes are inspired by the ikran

BEADED TOP

RESPECTED LEADER

Ikeyni was the strongest candidate for clan leader when her beloved husband, the *olo'eyktan*, died prematurely during a valiant hunt against a *nalutsa* bull that was terrorizing the cliffside *ikran* roost. Unprejudiced against female leaders, the clan supported her rise. Ikeyni won the ritual challenge fight, passed the trials, and was ceremonially confirmed.

Kuru

DATA FILE	
FULL NA'VI NAME	*Ikeyni te Vaka Tayingat'ite*
CLAN	Tayrangi
CLAN POSITION	*Olo'eykte*
BASE	Cliffs of the Eastern Sea

THE OMATIKAYA CLAN & ALLIES

FACT FILE

> Ikeyni has excellent tactical skills and has fought alongside Jake against the RDA more than any other clan leader.
> Ikeyni pushes herself to consistently strive for greatness, perfection, and harmony in her leadership role.
> Living on the coast, Ikeyni regularly dives for fish with her *ikran*.

Bone is attached to make headpiece more aerodynamic

IKRAN RIDING VISOR

Retains hide color of the tapiranax, a wild Pandoran boar that is prominent near the Eastern Sea cliffs

TAYRANGI LEGGINGS

IN LIFE AND DEATH
Repetition can be seen in Tayrangi songcord patterns, as they believe life is cyclical. They bury their dead in cliff nooks overlooking the waves. Small *ikran* consume the dead body, who in turn are consumed by larger *ikran*.

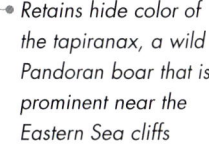
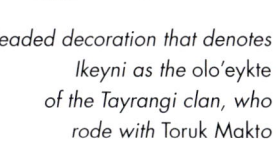
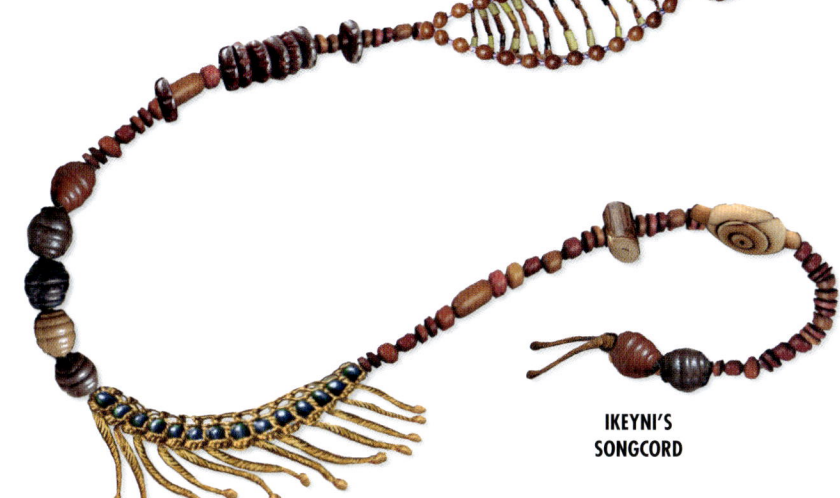

Beaded decoration that denotes Ikeyni as the olo'eykte of the Tayrangi clan, who rode with Toruk Makto

IKEYNI'S SONGCORD

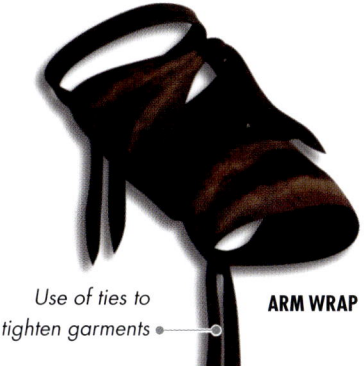

Use of ties to tighten garments

ARM WRAP

Finely woven

LOINCLOTH

AIRWEAR
As reknowned *ikran* aerialists, the Tayrangi tend to wear simple, streamlined garments to avoid impeding aerial flight.

THE TAYRANGI CLAN

The Tayrangi are known as the Ikran People of the Eastern Sea. The clan and its leader, Ikeyni, have a strong alliance with Jake Sully and the Omatikaya. Having fought alongside *Toruk Makto* during the Battle of the Hallelujah Mountains, the *ikran* warriors will not hesitate to answer Jake's call to battle the RDA again.

Ikeyni and the Tayrangi clan fly into battle against the RDA, with Jake and Neytiri leading the way.

THE METKAYINA CLAN

RECONCILING THE LOSS of Na'vi following the battle at Three Brothers Rocks, the Metkayina move forward with resilience and a deeper understanding of their situation. The reef clan knows war is upon them and their lives will be irrevocably changed. They must confront advanced warfare in ways that will challenge their belief system. However, this will not fundamentally alter their culture. In fact, it will strengthen it as they root themselves in traditions that reinforce their identity. Core values of clan continuity, connection, and kinship between themselves and the *tulkun* will endure. And their adherence to The Way of Water will guide them spiritually while they form new positive memories from celebrations, communions, and acts of selflessness.

METKAYINA VILLAGE LIFE

PROTECTED BY a natural sea wall, the Metkayina live on a tranquil island in harmony with the ocean. The predictable cycle of the tides shapes their daily life; low tide for gathering shells and seaweed, incoming tide for fishing, and high tide for returning to the village for community. The Reef People celebrate their connection with water through crafting, storytelling, and rituals like the Coming of Age ceremony, which they celebrate alongside their brethren *tulkun*. The Metkayina deeply respect the ocean, and in turn, the ocean provides them with everything they need.

WAVE MOTIFS
Inspired by water, the Metkayina weave patterns based on its forms, such as the rippling surface of the ocean.

LIVING TRADITION

Tradition shapes Metkayina identity, expressed through rituals, rites of passage, and art—such as clothing and tattoos. It gives young Metkayina a way to prove their worth and define their individuality, while elders uphold cultural norms. Some young Na'vi stray from tradition—for example, bonding with a *tulkun* before it is sanctioned—which can leave them isolated if seen as reckless. Yet Metkayina elders understand that personal conviction is sometimes like the ocean: it can soften barriers and bring about change. Their willingness to listen and adapt, while honoring tradition, has kept the clan strong for thousands of years.

One of the more beautiful and empowering experiences is the First Breath ceremony where the whole clan is present for the "water birth" of a Na'vi baby in the ocean.

VILLAGE COMMONS

The Metkayina Commons is a clan gathering pavillion at the heart of the village. Though primarily a central workspace for cooking and weaving rather than for ceremonial occasions, the Reef Na'vi will also gather beneath its canopy for group discussions, decision making, evening meals, and storytelling. And twice a year it functions as a central trading post for Wind Traders to set up goods for bartering. For an impressionable Na'vi child, the sight of the Commons is unforgettable, a symbol of clan unity, strength, and collective wisdom.

THE METKAYINA CLAN

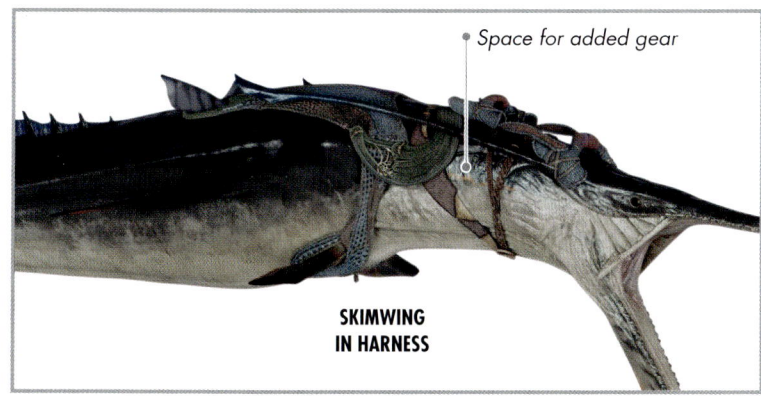

Space for added gear

SKIMWING IN HARNESS

METKAYINA TOOLS

Through thousands of years of evolution, the Reef People have evolved to use hunting tools that are designed for the ocean alone. These tools include crossbows, atlatls, and lances, all constructed from natural material. Metkayina youth are introduced to the fine art of fishing with this gear at an early age, while also learning how important it is to respect the ocean and to never take more than is needed.

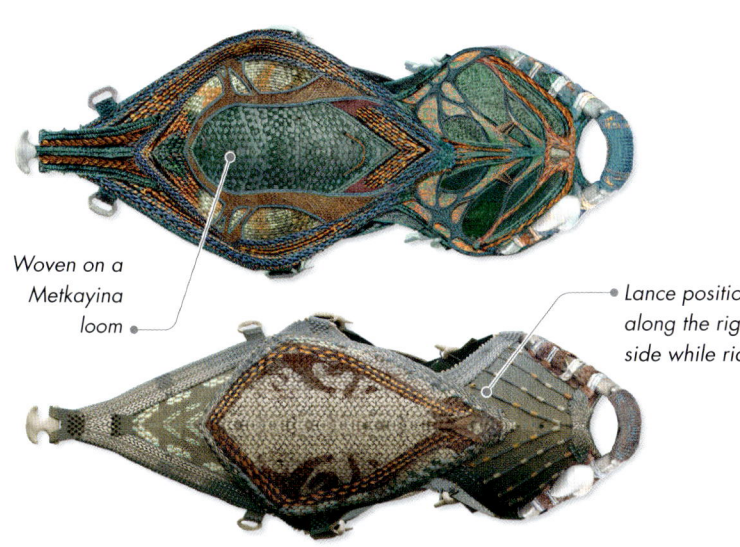

Woven on a Metkayina loom

Lance positioned along the right side while riding

ILU TACKS

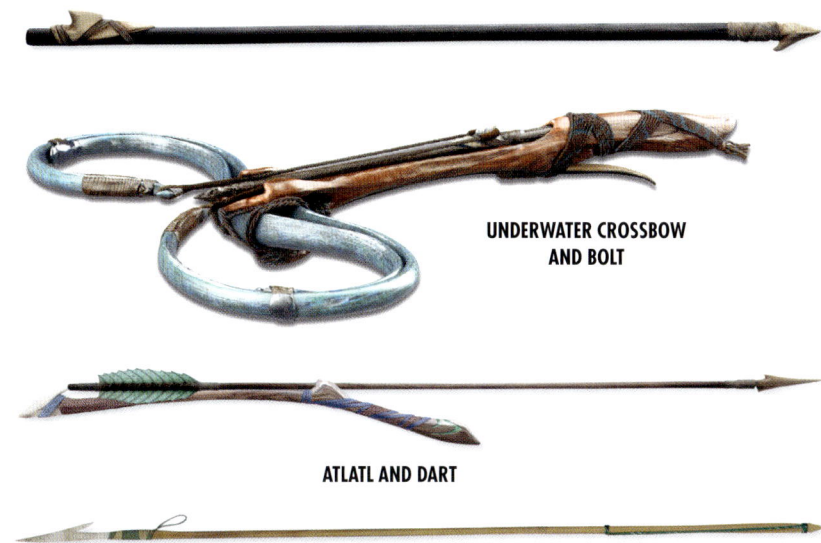

UNDERWATER CROSSBOW AND BOLT

ATLATL AND DART

POLE SPEAR

EMERGING PATTERNS
As a Na'vi matures, they transition from toys to tools that nurture their developing interests.

SKIMWING TACK

Colors and patterns personalized to the individual rider

Forms of sacred narratives

METKAYINA TATTOO MOTIFS

WATER DRUM

The Metkayina water drum is a large nautiloid shell played by Reef Na'vi during ceremonies. It is brought out of the water to be drained and capture air, then lowered, tethered to mangrove roots or coral structures, with its opening resting on the ocean floor to preserve the air cavity inside, like an air bell. From within, the drummer strikes a wide membrane, similar to a Terran taiko drum, generating a deep, resonant beat that carries through the water. It is notably used for the Coming of Age ceremony.

TONOWARI

TONOWARI IS THE BRAVE *olo'eyktan* of the Metkayina clan, the husband of pregnant *tsahik* Ronal, and father to two teenagers—his son, Ao'Nung, and daughter, Tsireya. He leads his People and represents them with the Tulkun Council. The *tulkun* clan of their archipelago live in close relationship with the Metkayina. Each reef child is paired with a *tulkun* infant calf at birth, and they maintain their relationship of Spirit Brother or Spirit Sister for life. Tonowari and Ronal are responsible for maintaining the harmony of this interspecies kinship, which is central to the culture of the Ocean Peoples of Pandora.

Symbolizes the sea wall

SHELL CHEST GUARD

Embedded abalone shells protect Tonowari's heart in battle, evocative of the strength found in the sea.

RISING TO THE CHALLENGE

After encountering the might of the RDA firsthand, Tonowari fully understands the grave threat the Na'vi and all life on Pandora face, especially their beloved *tulkun*, who are being systematically hunted with a fleet of killer ships. There is a bigger fight coming, a war that must unify all the clans, and Tonowari knows that the Metkayina will get drawn into it. At first afraid that Jake would bring the war to them, he now believes that Jake was sent to them by *Eywa* to lead them against the RDA. Tonowari begs Jake to fulfill the prophecy once again, to ride the great *toruk* and become *Toruk Makto*, the Rider of Last Shadow, uniter of the clans.

DATA FILE	
FULL NA'VI NAME	Tonowari te Tsika'u Arvak'itan
CLAN	Metkayina
CLAN POSITION	Olo'eyktan
BASE	Awa'atlu, a Metkayina reef village

ARMBAND

THE METKAYINA CLAN

BROTHER-IN-ARMS

Tonowari is the only person who understands Jake and the heavy burden of leadership. They are both men struggling to deal with their often-conflicting responsibilities toward their family and their community. Thanks to Tonowari, Jake, for the first time, truly comes to accept his twin roles — as a family man and also the one who must lead the Na'vi into battle.

FACT FILE

> Tonowari is honorable, open-minded, and reliable; a strong leader and warrior, and master diver and hunter.
> He is determined to oversee and protect the well-being of his family and clan whatever the cost.

MARUI TOTEM

KNIFE SHEATH
One of Tonowari's longest-held items

Braided akula skin

AKULA TOOTH MANTLE

THE COST OF VICTORY

With the help of the *tulkun* and rainforest Na'vi, Tonowari and his skimwing riders fight alongside *Toruk Makto* and neutralize the RDA threat, protecting their reef community. However, the victory comes at a grave cost. His wife, Ronal, dies in battle, though not before she delivers their baby daughter, Pril. Now a widowed father, his bond with Jake grows even stronger as they learn together how to cope with the grief of losing a loved one to war, while remaining focused on the needs and welfare of their families and People.

CEREMONIAL CLOAK

Tonowari's cloak was made by many Metkayina artisans and gifted to him in gratitude for his service as *olo'eyktan*. The design invokes his status as the central figure in the village latticework. A similar motif appears on the totem inside Tonowari's *marui*.

Handle and blade are one piece, wrapped for grip

An identifier of his status when riding in a large group of skimwings

Straight edge for cutting and shaping, serrated edge for splitting

KNIFE

FRINGED CAPELET

Piece from an old family canoe

TONOWARI'S SONGCORD

RONAL

DESPITE HAVING AVENGED her *tulkun* sister Roa's death at the battle of Three Brothers Rocks, Ronal is still resentful toward the Sully family. As *tsahìk* of the Metkayina, she prioritizes the well-being of her family and People, which has been threatened by the newcomers' arrival. Time-honored principles are tested as Jake Sully harbors weapons of metal and wants to train her People with them, which she vehemently opposes. However, she supports her husband's faith in Jake, albeit for the time being. If push comes to shove, however, she will not hesitate to do what is best for the clan and the future of her soon-to-be-born baby.

FACT FILE
> Ronal is independent, opinionated, influential, and also a fearsome warrior.
> Ronal will not hesitate to do what is best for the clan and the future of her soon-to-be-born baby.

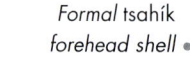
Crystal form of coral skeleton

Formal tsahìk forehead shell

CEREMONIAL SPEAR

Tattoo framing the stomach

Skirt paired with top as gown

SMUDGE STICK SHELL BOWL

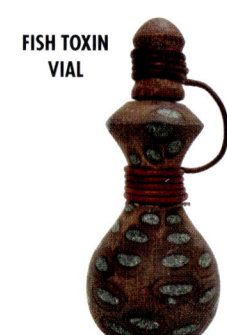
FISH TOXIN VIAL

HEALING ABILITIES

As *tsahìk*, Ronal provides her People with spiritual guidance and the healing arts of a shaman, using plant medicines and the protective power of *Eywa* (all nature is a single connected system, and that system is a manifestation of *Eywa*). She has a kit consisting of sharp quills dipped in extracts from plants and ocean animals, smudge sticks made of her healing herbs for purification, and poultices containing plant-derived oils for treating wounds. She is highly respected and relied upon by her People.

As the alpha female of the reef clan, Ronal is threatened by Neytiri's strong personality and status as a near-legendary warrior. Tension builds between them — even though Neytiri is determined to earn her keep.

THE METKAYINA CLAN

CEREMONIAL LEADER

Ronal presides over the Coming of Age ceremony in which young Na'vi and *tulkun* receive their first tattoo (*tolu*) on the side of their faces. The reef teenagers' *tulkun* brothers and sisters also receive their first *tolu*, applied by Na'vi artists. This mark represents their family name and patronymic or matronymic name—including the name of their *tulkun* or Na'vi brother or sister—and symbolizes a first step into adulthood. After the tattoo is administered with a fish-spine needle, Ronal uses a wet sea sponge to wipe away any residual ink, revealing the design and the individual's unique identity and self-expression to all.

Cord acts as an ink reservoir

TATTOO KIT

SEA SPONGE

DATA FILE	
FULL NA'VI NAME	Ronal te Natsira Tan'ite
CLAN	Metkayina
CLAN POSITION	Tsahik
BASE	Awa'atlu, a Metkayina reef village

The forehead tattoo is her first

Birth of Tsireya

KNIFE

All-purpose blade

Chest guard

PRIL

RECONCILIATION

Ronal blames Neytiri and her family for bringing war to their People. They spar verbally and hiss at each other, but never come to blows. As encroachment by the RDA escalates, petty grievances fade to the background. In the battle at the Cove of the Ancestors, Ronal's heroic attacks lead to her being mortally wounded in the underwater battle. Neytiri rescues her from drowning and reluctantly turns away from returning to the fight herself in order to stand guard over Ronal while she gives birth in her final minutes of life. Neytiri promises the dying Ronal she will protect the newborn Pril, which proves easier said than done, given the challenges still ahead of Neytiri in the battle.

SONGCORD

41

TSIREYA

PATIENT AND INDEPENDENT-MINDED, Tsireya is the young *tsakarem* of the Metkayina, destined to succeed her mother Ronal and become *tsahik*. In the aftermath of the battle at Three Brothers Rocks, Tsireya feels that Lo'ak is right about Payakan's moral code, because the young *tulkun* bull saved her life when she was a prisoner on the SeaDragon ship. But she also respects the pacifistic *tulkun* way—so she's torn between her parents' beliefs and what she knows in her heart to be true. Payakan's fate is decided by the Tulkun Council of Elders and he is exiled. Lo'ak protests, confronting Tonowari, Ronal, and the entire clan, resulting in Tsireya's parents forbidding her to speak with him. She usually follows their rules, but this time she refuses.

• Leaves from nearby mangrove forest

LOINCLOTH

BRAIDED SHELL ARMBAND

TIES THAT BIND

Tsireya remains at Lo'ak's side as he comes to terms with the death of his brother, Neteyam. She encourages him to repair his mother's ancestral war bow, broken in battle with the RDA, sensing that it has a powerful symbolic value. Once finished, the bow is as strong as ever. It inspires Lo'ak to find his inner strength and reinforces the strong connection he shares with Tsireya.

• Pearl headband

• Loincloth with decorative seashells

Tsireya rides with Lo'ak as they greet the Wind Traders.

THE METKAYINA CLAN

TSIREYA'S SONGCORD

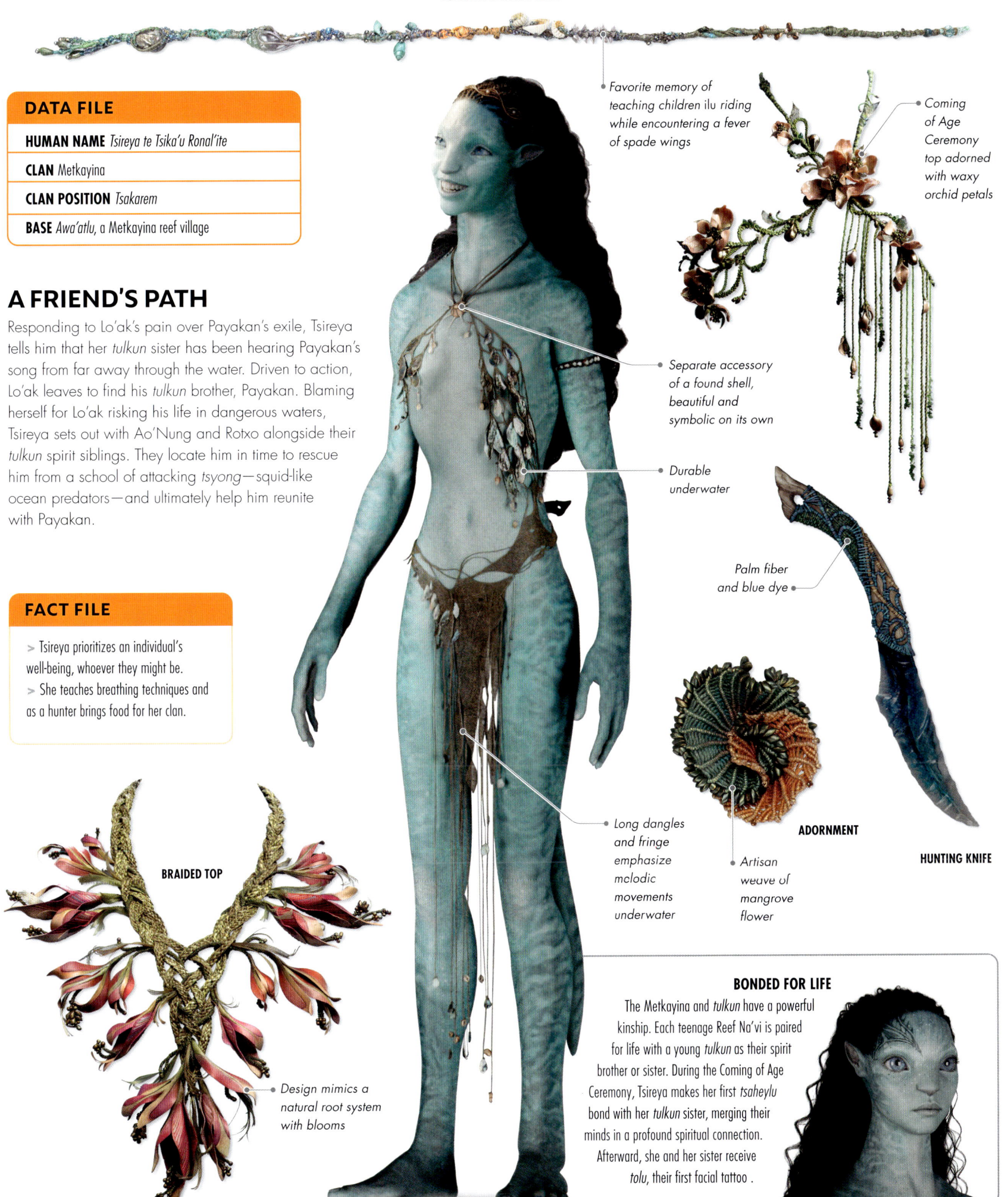

- Favorite memory of teaching children ilu riding while encountering a fever of spade wings
- Coming of Age Ceremony top adorned with waxy orchid petals
- Separate accessory of a found shell, beautiful and symbolic on its own
- Durable underwater
- Palm fiber and blue dye
- Long dangles and fringe emphasize melodic movements underwater
- Artisan weave of mangrove flower
- Design mimics a natural root system with blooms

BRAIDED TOP

ADORNMENT

HUNTING KNIFE

DATA FILE

HUMAN NAME Tsireya te Tsika'u Ronal'ite
CLAN Metkayina
CLAN POSITION Tsakarem
BASE Awa'atlu, a Metkayina reef village

A FRIEND'S PATH

Responding to Lo'ak's pain over Payakan's exile, Tsireya tells him that her *tulkun* sister has been hearing Payakan's song from far away through the water. Driven to action, Lo'ak leaves to find his *tulkun* brother, Payakan. Blaming herself for Lo'ak risking his life in dangerous waters, Tsireya sets out with Ao'Nung and Rotxo alongside their *tulkun* spirit siblings. They locate him in time to rescue him from a school of attacking *tsyong*—squid-like ocean predators—and ultimately help him reunite with Payakan.

FACT FILE

> Tsireya prioritizes an individual's well-being, whoever they might be.
> She teaches breathing techniques and as a hunter brings food for her clan.

BONDED FOR LIFE

The Metkayina and *tulkun* have a powerful kinship. Each teenage Reef Na'vi is paired for life with a young *tulkun* as their spirit brother or sister. During the Coming of Age Ceremony, Tsireya makes her first *tsaheylu* bond with her *tulkun* sister, merging their minds in a profound spiritual connection. Afterward, she and her sister receive *tolu*, their first facial tattoo.

AO'NUNG

AO'NUNG IS HEADSTRONG, aware that other young Na'vi look up to him in times of uncertainty. His relationship with the Sully kids has improved—he no longer sees them as ignorant outsiders—and it deepens with Lo'ak. They relate strongly to one another, owing to the pressures placed upon them by their respective parents, as well as the tragic death of Neteyam. Ao'Nung seeks to improve himself as a young leader, sensing that Lo'ak will rise to become one, too. And what better time to form a bond with a lifelong ally than now?

DATA FILE
- **FULL NA'VI NAME** Ao'Nung te Tsika'u Tonowari'itan
- **CLAN** Metkayina
- **CLAN POSITION** Son of *olo'eytkan*, hunter/diver
- **BASE** Awa'atlu, a Metkayina reef village

AO'NUNG'S KNIFE AND SHEATH
- Skimwing jawbone blade

LOINCLOTH
- Sourced from a seagrass bed

NECKLACE
- Marine ikran talon wrapped in fish-scale leather

SHELL ARMBAND
- Iridescent shell chips washed ashore

- Chest guard with decorated armored akula plates
- Braided fringe loincloth

COMING OF AGE

Ao'Nung and other Reef teens participate in a one-on-one coming-of-age ritual with the *tulkun*. In this ancient ceremony, a Na'vi child bonds with a chosen *tulkun*, creating a sibling-like spiritual connection that lasts a lifetime and is deeply meaningful to both ocean Na'vi and the *tulkun*. Their cultures are intertwined, and at the end of the ceremony, Ao'Nung receives his first *tolu*, marking the shared story between him and his brother *tulkun*. From his proud parents he also receives a woven chest guard, symbolic of his coming of age and becoming "Brother of Tulkun." He will wear it with pride, as all young Na'vi adults do after their rite of passage.

FACT FILE
> Ao'Nung is staunchly loyal to family, friends, and Metkayina culture.
> He is a natural leader and hunter who commands respect from his peers.

ROTXO

A TEENAGE NA'VI male hunter/diver of the Metkayina, Rotxo is a constant companion to Ao'Nung and Tsireya. He has a naturally sunny disposition and is excited to embrace the Omatikayan newcomers and their half-Sky-People children. Rotxo has a lot to learn as he approaches adulthood, but by surrounding himself with children like those of noble clan leaders and the Sully family, he is on the right path to become a worthy Metkayina. Alongside Ao'Nung and Tsireya, he helps teach the Sully kids to dive, ride *ilu* and skimwings, body surf the reef tunnels and embrace ocean life. He takes an interest in Kiri, who's not quite sure what to make of his attention. She studiously listens to what Rotxo has to teach, and he is happy to have her company.

FACT FILE
> Rotxo helped Ao'Nung and other hunters recover the akula body that attacked Lo'ak, for clan resources.
> He is determined to uphold the ideals of the Metkayina clan.

DATA FILE
FULL NA'VI NAME	Rotxo te Rara Yapto'itan
CLAN	Metkayina
CLAN POSITION	Hunter/diver
BASE	Awa'atlu, a Metkayina reef village

A NOBLE DEATH

With a courage that reflects the finest Metkayina warriors, Rotxo rides his *ilu* out against the boats and subs that are hunting the *tulkun* mothers and calves. He successfully attacks the boat crews with his spear-fishing crossbow, but is hit by several rounds from a Crab Suit's rotary speargun. Ao'Nung, Tsireya and the Sully kids mourn his heroic sacrifice.

TOTEMS
Scales gifted by Rotxo's fisher parents, a reminder of their love and belief in him.

KNIFE

Chest guard decorated with cephalopod bone

ROTXO'S SONG
While other adolescents rebelled, Rotxo followed expectations —far from perfect, but with growing awareness of the hierarchies around him and how to move through them in ways that helped others.

Carved from a Wind Trader bead, inspired by how an individual's life can impact others through story

Seagrass from the lagoon shallows

ROTXO'S SONGCORD

COVE OF THE ANCESTORS

THE COVE OF THE ANCESTORS is a sacred site and sanctuary for the Metkayina that serves many cultural purposes. It resides within one of several powerful fluxcons (flux concentrations) on Pandora, an intense magnetic field where a high concentration of unobtanium forms a superconducting amplifier for the exo-moon's already powerful magnetic force. At the Cove of the Ancestors, massive arches of ferrous rock have formed following the flux lines, similar to the sacred arches at the Tree of Souls. This majestic landmark is also scattered with floating islands of different heights, above and below the ocean surface, where deposits of unobtanium levitate the rocks in the powerful magnetic fields. This is a manifestation of the Meisner effect, or "flux pinning," also known as magnetic levitation, caused by the superconducting properties of unobtanium—the only known naturally occurring room-temperature superconductor.

CALF COMMUNION CEREMONY

In the cove is a large blue hole, and central to that is a magnificent underwater Spirit Tree or, as the Na'vi call it, *Ranteng Utralti*. The Na'vi connect with the spirit world through the fronds of the tree to commune with the stored memories of their ancestors. This is where the Calf Communion ceremony is held, attended by Reef Na'vi and their bonded *tulkun* brothers and sisters.

THE METKAYINA CLAN

SEA CAVES

Along the shores of the Cove of the Ancestors are limestone sea caves that tides have created over time. Natural labyrinths have formed with deep tunnels, serving as bunker-like shelters. They are used for ceremonies and also function as gathering places for storytelling. Such caves are commonly found throughout the reef and often provide dwellings for the ocean clans.

FACT FILE

› Several species of flora exist in the Cove of the Ancestors, including hanging vines on the floating islands.
› Sometimes at night, a purple and cyan aurora appears above the Cove of the Ancestors.

FLUX DEVIL

TWIN SPIRALS of energy wrapped around each other, the Flux Devil twists vertically more than 3,000 feet (914.4 m) in the air above the entrance to the Cove of the Ancestors. Water, a diamagnetic fluid, is levitated by the hugely powerful magnetic fields, curling upward in spiraling inverted waterfalls. Additionally, eerie cyan and purple plasma flows follow the helical flux. It is called the Flux Devil by humans due to its whirlwind formation, reminiscent of Terran dust devils. No metal can be carried or worn inside the Flux Devil, as the magnetic field is so strong that it will be torn away. However, native plants are fine and animals are safe for short periods.

BLAZING INFERNO

The gases in fire, such as water vapor and carbon dioxide, are diamagnetic. When the Factory Ship explodes beneath Quaritch and Spider at the Flux Devil, the flames are visibly bent by the magnetic field, repelled along the path of least resistance.

THE METKAYINA CLAN

THE OCEAN OF PANDORA

SEEN FROM ABOVE, Pandora's ocean appears as a blue bed stretching to the horizon. But beneath its surface, coral branches, seagrass, and macroalgae form meadows much like those on land—every element interconnected, each part sustaining the other. When entering this world, as the Reef Na'vi do, life abounds, from the friendly, otter-like *zukzuk* greeting guests to the dangerous akula lurking for a meal. Deeper still, near thermal vents, dwell *tsyong*, creatures of darkness that communicate through bioluminescence. And then there are the *tulkun*—a highly intelligent species whose cultural and intellectual development matches that of the Na'vi. They possess names, rich family histories, and a sophisticated appreciation of the arts, from music to poetry. Together, the Reef Na'vi and the *tulkun* find common ground in the ocean, sharing ceremonies and spiritual connection—a vibrant community of wonders amid vast biodiversity that shows just how alive the ocean world truly is.

TULKUN COUNCIL OF ELDERS

THE TULKUN COUNCIL OF ELDERS is a ruling body comprising older *tulkun* that carry the wisdom of their ancestral history and make decisions on all matters related to the pods in their region (The Eastern Sea). These include resource allocation, migration routes, coming-of-age honors, Na'vi relations, conflict resolution (adhering to absolute pacifism), and in extremely rare instances, infractions caused by a *tulkun*. The council may consist of elders from one pod, such as the Metkayina's group, or several, depending on the importance of the decisions to be made. Much like the Na'vi Council of Elders, the *tulkun* do not have a single, all-powerful leader; they prefer consensus. The council is trusted and respected by both the *tulkun* and Reef Na'vi. Any Na'vi permitted to participate in an assembly must be accompanied by their *olo'eytkan* or *olo'eykte*.

FACT FILE

> During council with Na'vi, *tulkun* elders spyhop above the water in a circle for several minutes at a time.
> A typical council is made up of 8 to 10 *tulkun* elders.

CEREMONIAL DRESS

For councils and ceremonies, Reef Na'vi adorn their brethren *tulkun* matriarch and patriarchs with body rings and colorful, woven streamers, signifiers of rank and ceremony. This ornamentation honors the commitment the Metkayina clan and *tulkun* pod have to each other and emphasizes the continuing importance of their shared history. Na'vi weavers devote much care to creating the streamers, whose designs—unique for each individual—have deep meaning for both the Na'vi and *tulkun* participants in their joint ceremonies and celebrations.

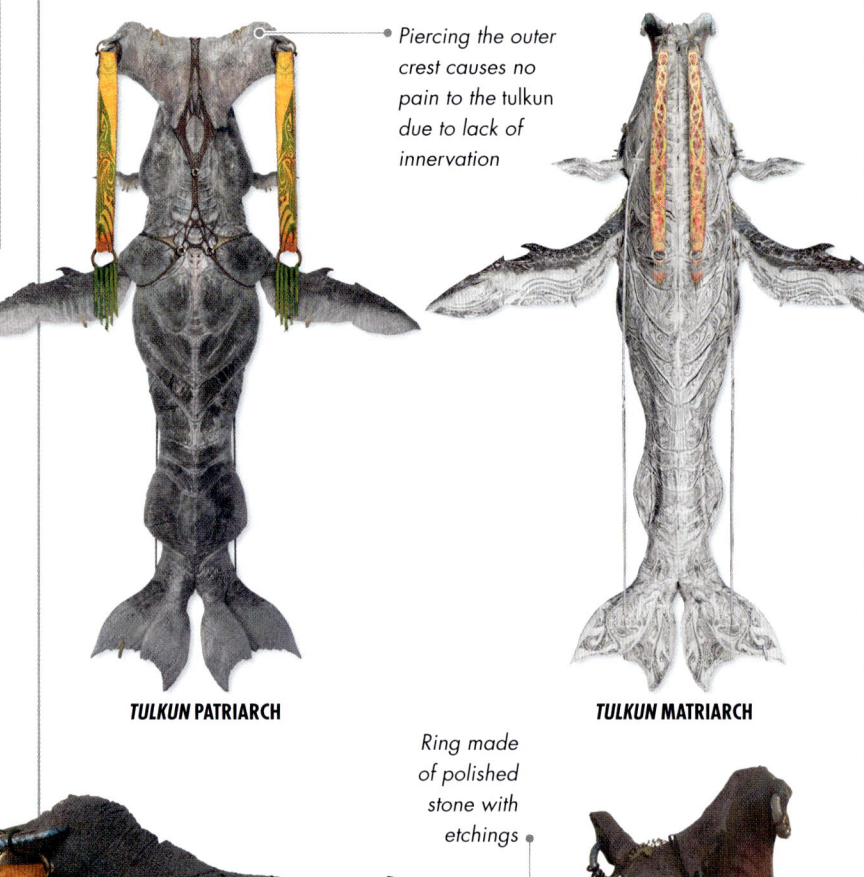

Piercing the outer crest causes no pain to the tulkun due to lack of innervation

TULKUN PATRIARCH

TULKUN MATRIARCH

Ring made of polished stone with etchings

Streamer crafted from woven rattan

THE OCEAN OF PANDORA

TA'NOK

Found by Payakan as the last of his birth clan, which was wiped out by the RDA in their quest to harvest *tulkun amrita*, Ta'nok is a powerful female who rose up against the hunting ships that killed her children and her People. Scarred and blinded from her stand against the RDA's weapons, she speaks for the dead calves and the dead mothers, and all the songs of her People, now gone forever.

Tattered lift bag still attached to an RDA harpoon line

One of several deeply embedded RDA harpoons

The last remnant of her family name.

THE TRIAL OF PAYAKAN

Payakan is a rogue *tulkun* who has been rejected by his pod. He is considered an outcast by the reef community for inciting young bulls to fight the RDA for hunting *tulkun*, resulting in the loss of *tulkun*, as well as Na'vi, lives. Payakan is brought to trial before the Tulkun Council of Elders for his actions and is exiled. However, his spirit brother Lo'ak and friend Ta'nok—the only member of her pod to survive the RDA attack by fighting back—advocate for the council to do the same. Convinced by Ta'nok, who gives a voice to the dead calves and mothers killed by the RDA, the Tulkun Council agrees to join the fight.

Cephalic fin, maimed in Payakan's first confrontation with the RDA

TSYONG

DEEP-WATER PREDATORS, the *tsyong* share physical similarities to Terran squid but with notable differences: shark and stingray-like fins, intakes resembling engines on the side with siphons on the underside for propulsion, multiple eyes, and two long tentacles ending in elongated digits with finger-like grips. *Tsyong* communicate using bioluminescent chromatophores made up of millions of pigment cells and can give stunning displays when they are "chattering" or orchestrating a coordinated attack. The changing colors of these cells also provide them with camouflage for hunting and defense.

DATA FILE

NAME Southern Squidray

NA'VI NAME *Tsyong*

TAXONOMY *Velociteuthis mortigravis* or "swift deadly squid"

HABITAT Oceans of Pandora

ANATOMY Squid-like with sharp-toothed beaks.

FACT FILE

> *Tsyong*s' bioluminescent chromatophores have a muscle built into them, allowing these invertebrates to change color at lightning speed.
> The *tsyong* navigates blind spots by swiftly shifting on its axis.

The *tsyong* engage in cooperative hunting strategies, primarily using shrouding tactics to confuse prey.

UP FROM THE DEPTHS

Tsyong live deep underwater around a hydrothermal vent system. The area contains a swarming biomass, including clam-like organisms that *tsyong* like to eat. The *tsyong*'s large, squid-like eyes enable it to see clearly in darkness and, at night in shallow waters, detect lurking predators such as the akula. It can move forward and backward effortlessly using its siphons to propel itself, as well as compress its tentacles into a torpedo shape for rapid underwater movement. Smart and fast, *tsyong* hunt in packs. In attacks against RDA Crab Suits or Makos, they swarm out of the darkness, seize the submersibles with their tentacles and rip, rupture, or yank pieces off the vessels with their powerful beaks. They are able to smash through the canopies of Makos and Crab Suits, and extract the occupants. Their jet siphons allow them to leap far out of the water, and with lighting-fast tentacles, they grasp and pull themselves rapidly up ship's ramps and across decks. RDA crews have no chance against their rapacious onslaught.

• Powerful suckers for holding onto prey

BEAUTY IN DARKNESS

An RDA marine biologist once observed a *tsyong* shimmering through clouds of water rising from hydrothermal vents, its bioluminescence pulsing and reflecting off the vapor, creating a dreamlike atmosphere.

THE OCEAN OF PANDORA

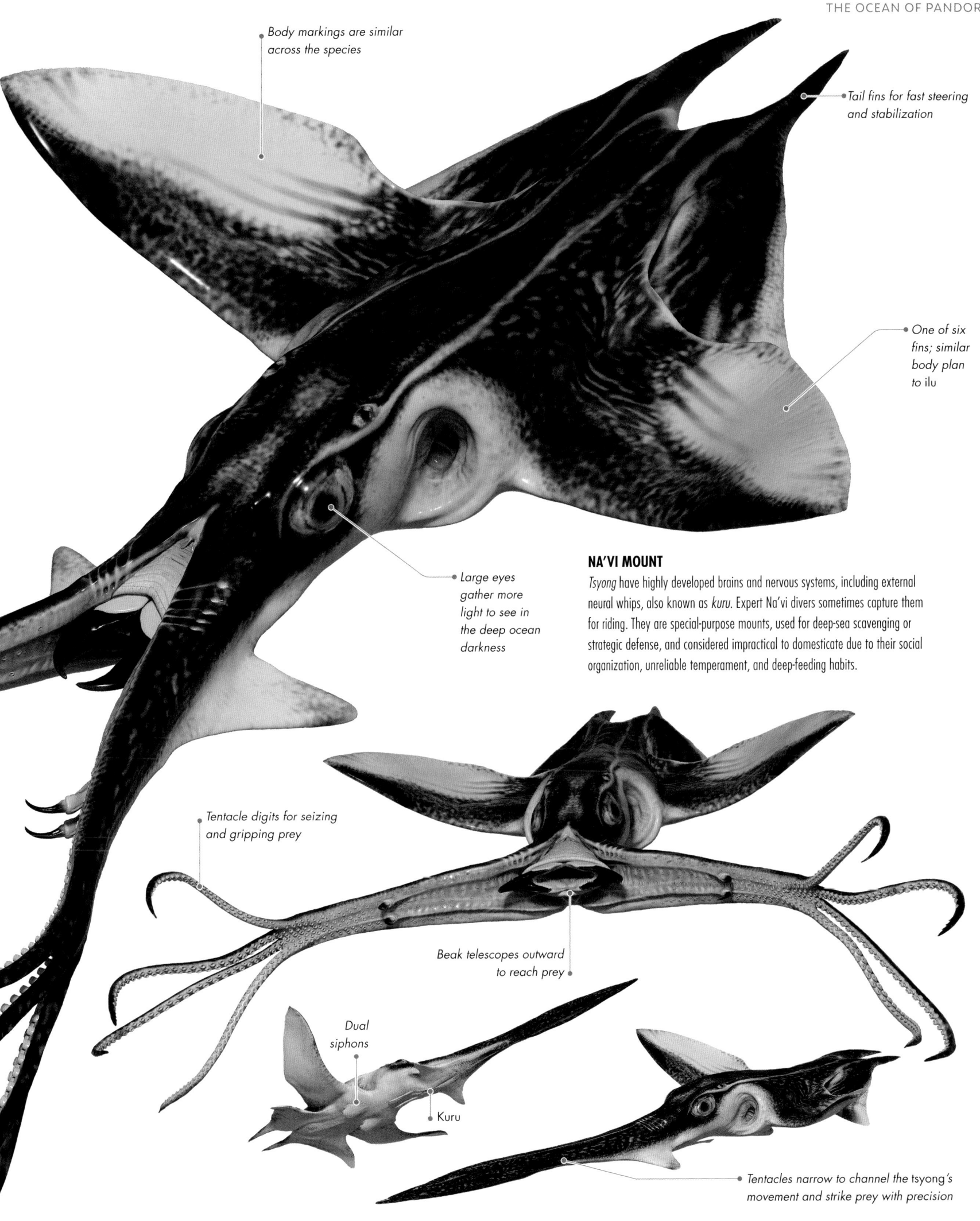

Body markings are similar across the species

Tail fins for fast steering and stabilization

One of six fins; similar body plan to ilu

Large eyes gather more light to see in the deep ocean darkness

NA'VI MOUNT

Tsyong have highly developed brains and nervous systems, including external neural whips, also known as *kuru*. Expert Na'vi divers sometimes capture them for riding. They are special-purpose mounts, used for deep-sea scavenging or strategic defense, and considered impractical to domesticate due to their social organization, unreliable temperament, and deep-feeding habits.

Tentacle digits for seizing and gripping prey

Beak telescopes outward to reach prey

Dual siphons

Kuru

Tentacles narrow to channel the tsyong's movement and strike prey with precision

ZUKZUK

THE ZUKZUK, or Pandoran otterfin, is an amphibious marine mammal known for its nimble swimming ability and playful behavior with other species, including the Na'vi. Highly social, it has distinct flaps along the armor plating of its back that, in addition to dispersing heat, are used for communication. It can open these flaps to appear larger for defense or to draw attention from potential mates. When the flaps close deliberately, they produce a clapping sound to alert nearby otterfins of potential threats or resources above or below the ocean surface. The sound also functions as a form of social reinforcement, signaling trust and affection. The same also applies to the flaps opening and closing to form bubbles. Though the otterfin lives primarily in water, it can be seen eating or resting on rocks and beaches.

The otterfin often demonstrates curiousity.

DATA FILE	
NAME	Pandoran otterfin
NA'VI NAME	Zukzuk (zook-zook)
TAXONOMY	*Enhydra pinnilutris* or "finned otter"
HABITAT	Waters of Pandora
ANATOMY	Otter-like with fins and armor flaps

Fins can fan out as needed or form a single shape

Flexible armor-plated flaps

VISIBLE TRAITS

The otterfin sits in the middle of the food chain as both predator and prey. It can protrude its teeth to clamp onto and pry open hard-shelled creatures like crustaceans and clams. It is believed to have evolved from land and adapted to water, as suggested by its hand-like paws and skeletal digits within its limbs and fins—combined features that are uncommon in Pandoran sea life. Scientists are actively investigating its origins, as the otterfin is known to appear in a variety of colors across Pandora depending on its environment, a trait that may inform local adaptations and broader evolutionary patterns.

Mouth opens in four directions

Hand-like paws for climbing and eating

Able to breathe underwater for up to 10 minutes.

The *zukzuk* can use its paws to pull open crustacean shells.

AKULA

THE AKULA is a fearsome marine apex predator with razor-sharp teeth, segmented body armor, and a voracious appetite. It is a monster from the deep, a true leviathan. Because it does not breathe air, it can lie in wait adopting an ambush strategy, silent like a Terran great white shark. It is not uncommon to see *ilu*, *skimwing*, and juvenile *tulkun* lifted clear out of the water by an akula strike from below. Even low-flying marine *ikran* are prey for the surface-to-air missile of the akula. Its stripes aid camouflage from above, imitating the ways the rays of Pandora's suns strike the ocean surface.

DATA FILE

NAME	Akula
NA'VI NAME	*Pxazang*
TAXONOMY	*Tyranichthis bernardi* or "tyrannical fish"
HABITAT	Oceans of Pandora
ANATOMY	Trifurcated mouth, razor sharp teeth, segmented, patterned body armor

- White stripes or saddle patches trace the creature's spine and fins
- Flexible armor of segmented plates run along body

FACT FILE

> The akula's flexible plate armor provides protection from attack and unrestricted mobility.
> Its teeth are composed of silica with geothite fibers along the edges—perhaps the hardest substance ever discovered on Pandora.
> The animal has a bite force of 10,000 psi (703.01 kgf/cm^2) and the ability to control the torque of its jaws for maximum power.

THREE JAWS
One of the akula's most remarkable features is its trifurcated mouth, which consists of two top jaws and one bottom jaw filled with black teeth. To see around it when its mouth is fully open, the akula has secondary eyes on protruding stalks.

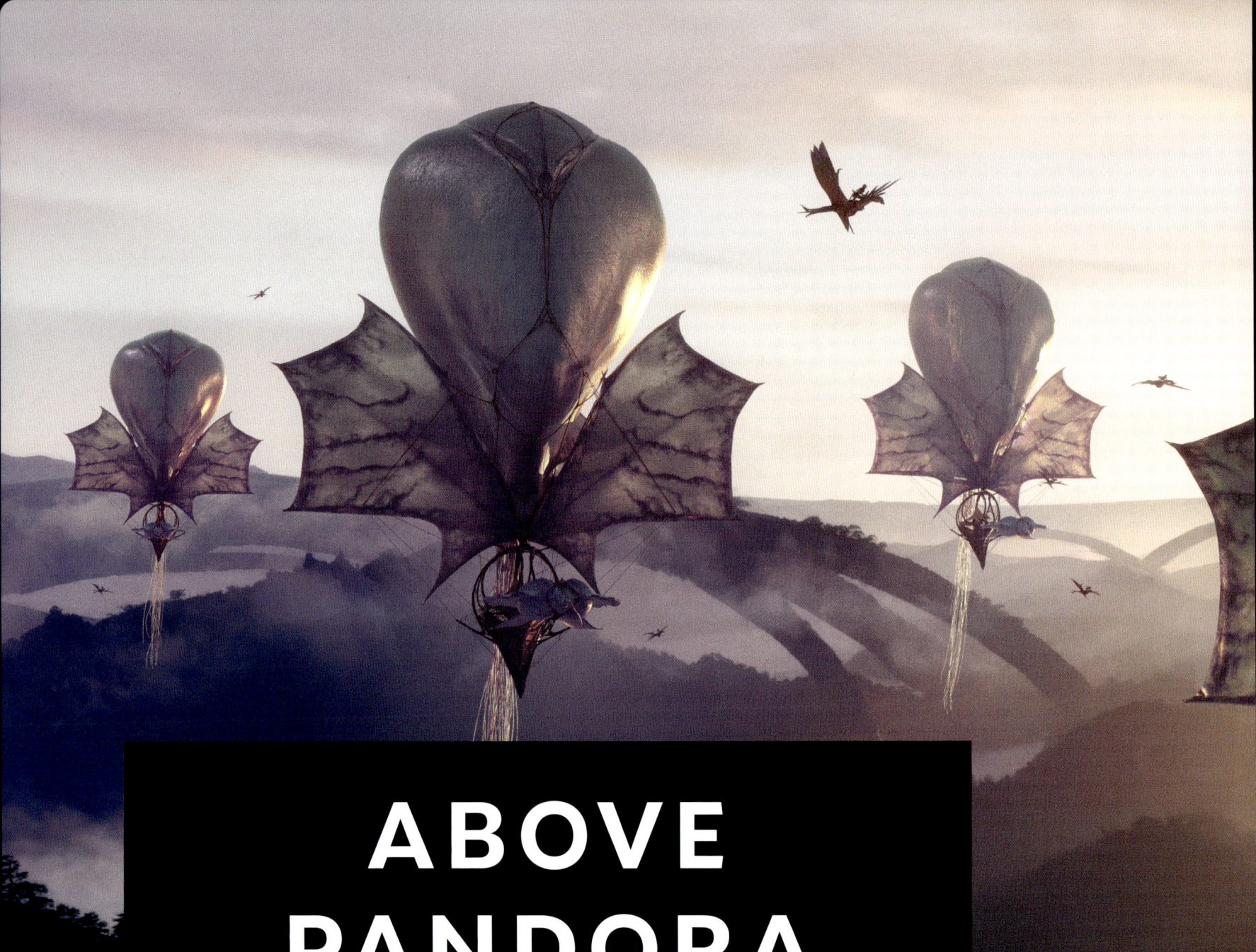

ABOVE PANDORA

AS THE WIND TRADERS SAY, "Praise be to *Eywa* for kind wind and fair weather," when viewing Pandora's breathtaking vistas from the skies. Migrating hammerheads move in vast herds through shallow wetlands below, while winged tetrapterons glide over low stone arches ribboned with trees. At night, bioluminescence laces the ground as a network of light and living energy. Like a gem on a Na'vi songcord, these sights are stories, sung and treasured, unique to the individual and a reflection of their identity. All of Pandora can never be fully explored, and its richness cannot be experienced in single lifetime, but it is enough to fill one completely. A limitless ascension of the spirit awaits those who embrace the adventures that lie beyond the horizon.

THE TLALIM CLAN

DATA FILE
NA'VI NAME *Tlalim* (tlah'-leem)
RANGE (BIOME) Nomadic (aerial) throughout tropical and temperate climates.
BEHAVIOR Self-sufficient, resourceful, adventurous, highly social.
LANGUAGE Na'vi dialect

THE TLALIM, commonly known as the Wind Traders, sail the skies in convoys of elegantly-woven gondolas held aloft by giant jellyfish-like medusoids—living hydrogen gas bags with long tentacles. The Wind Traders have harnessed these animals to lift their aerial ships, whose agile crews use long reins to rotate the medusoids' steering vanes in flight. While most Na'vi clans prioritize hunting and gathering for their livelihood, this clan has adapted to become sharp and resourceful traders. They are highly social, famous for their love of bartering, and great tellers of news, tall tales, and gossip.

Breathable fabric lets in air and moisture to help regulate body temperature across climates

SKIRT

TRINKETS

FLYING IN STYLE

Wind Traders favor exotic beads, stones, and crystals worn over rich and colorful textiles. The articles adorning their bodies hail from a vast array of locations—from the towering rock formations of the Southern Highlands to the grassy plains of the Western Veldt—each one possessing its unique story and significance. They also dress practically, donning thick cloaks to keep warm from wind and weather at high altitudes. Wind Traders weave their textiles on portable hand looms conducive to nomadic life, which is why many of their textiles are patchworked together to create larger pieces.

Chest adornment gifted by Peylak to his mate, Yu'nar, emphasizing strong heart

FORM AND FUNCTION

Wind Trader clothes are crafted for expression and functionality. Adorned shoulder pieces secure cloaks against strong winds.

Constructed in either leather or alternative fabric

ARM WRAPS

Hollow, bamboo-like pieces

BANGLES

Traditionally worn in matching pairs along the legs or arms, bangles are lightweight for everyday use, or embellished with beads for dancing. More grooves and ridges typically denote greater seniority.

Wind Trader Na'vi dance to music performed on a wide range of instruments from all over Pandora.

ABOVE PANDORA

A signaler announces the arrival of the Wind Traders with a resonating, horn-like whistle.

BRINGING THE NEWS
Everywhere they go, Wind Traders bring stories of other Na'vi cultures, as well as receiving local messages and tales to pass on during their travels. This news-gathering supplements *Eywa*'s neural network. Occasionally, it is told through song and music.

Arrow deer hide from the Zeswa clan

STANDING DRUM

PERSONAL EFFECTS
A Wind Trader is admired not only for the breadth of their adornments, but also for the novelty of each piece and the joy they bring, tributes to their adventurous spirit.

CUMMERBUND AND BREECHCLOTH (SKIRT)

WAIST WRAPS

Secures skirts; pads body during load-bearing or rigging, aids knot work, and doubles as lashing if needed

WIND INSTRUMENT

Air from the blowing tube reaches pipes fitted with free reed

Often worn by dancers for the rhythmic sound of clanking beads

ARMBAND

Keeps kuru in place during high winds

KURU CHEST PIECE

Broken kernel from a tranquil seed

Small and light enough to carry and perform at a market

HAND DRUM

SEASONED TRAVELERS
Because the Wind Traders fly by way of the trade winds, some of which are seasonal, they usually circumnavigate Pandora twice a year. They meet many clans, and so have a broader perspective on life compared to their Na'vi brethren. This has led the Wind Traders to develop a culture based on awareness, acceptance, and inclusivity. They understand and respect other clan customs. Always on the move, Wind Traders are not averse to new company on a long journey, but such favors must be creatively negotiated. Under the right circumstances, they will exchange a trip for *sarenyu*, a meaningful story that comes from the heart.

Ikran *in the clouds*

Ikran *protecting the flotilla among the stars*

TEA GOURDS

A WIND TRADER MARKET

THE TLALIM WIND TRADERS ply their trade between Pandora's diverse Na'vi cultures, setting up a market at each destination—usually a Na'vi village—exchanging exotic fruits and vegetables, dried meat, as well as tools, textiles, and trinkets. The Wind Traders' arrival usually signals a feast and dancing. However, not all of Pandora is available for the Wind Traders to visit. Certain territories are off limits, especially the colder regions, where their medusoids could start to ice up and get too heavy to fly.

A FAIR EXCHANGE

The Wind Traders live by bartering—money does not exist among the Na'vi. The premise of the Na'vi bartering system is that everybody benefits from a shared exchange. The Wind Traders, for example, gladly accept supplies of fresh food—much needed when traveling the skies. Because the Wind Traders fly mostly by way of the trade winds, they circumnavigate Pandora twice a year. This allows them to barter goods that are considered rare or out of season by other clans.

BASE MATERIALS

INDIVIDUALLY CRAFTED

The Na'vi trade raw materials to create meaningful adornments for themselves. Wind Traders often craft *ikran* motifs into trinkets for their clothing.

TEXTILE

Shaped into an ikran kuru

MARKET NECKLACE

Wind Trader keepsake, usually gifted

TRINKET

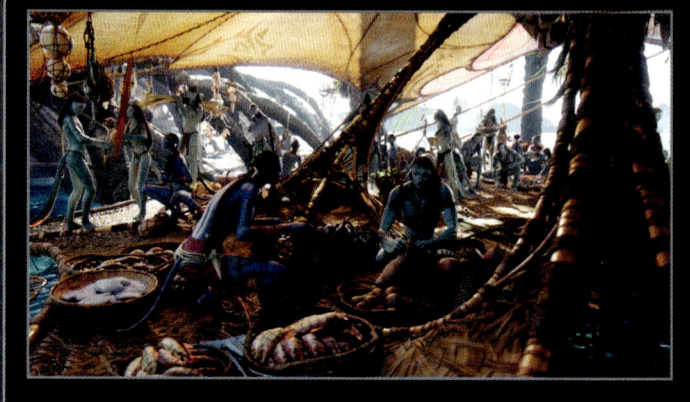

A trader offers goods and tools that help other Na'vi maintain their way of life.

ABOVE PANDORA

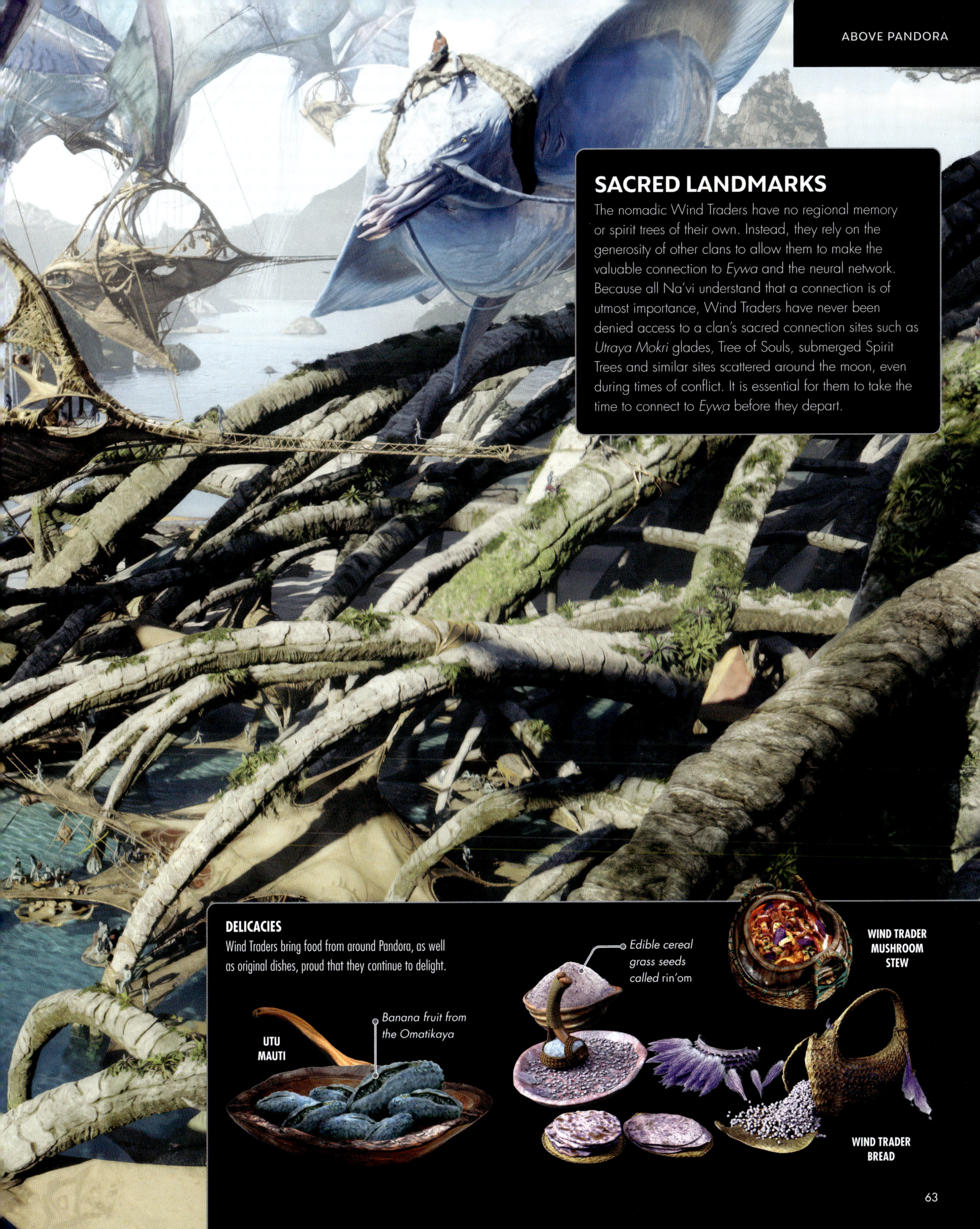

SACRED LANDMARKS

The nomadic Wind Traders have no regional memory or spirit trees of their own. Instead, they rely on the generosity of other clans to allow them to make the valuable connection to *Eywa* and the neural network. Because all Na'vi understand that a connection is of utmost importance, Wind Traders have never been denied access to a clan's sacred connection sites such as *Utraya Mokri* glades, Tree of Souls, submerged Spirit Trees and similar sites scattered around the moon, even during times of conflict. It is essential for them to take the time to connect to *Eywa* before they depart.

DELICACIES

Wind Traders bring food from around Pandora, as well as original dishes, proud that they continue to delight.

UTU MAUTI

Banana fruit from the Omatikaya

Edible cereal grass seeds called rin'om

WIND TRADER MUSHROOM STEW

WIND TRADER BREAD

WIND TRADERS' GONDOLA

THE WIND TRADERS FLY in a convoy of five to eight gondolas. Each one has a crew of 20 to 30 Na'vi organized by family bonds. Leading them is the *olo'eyktan*, who oversees life on all the gondolas like the admiral of a fleet, as well as captaining his own gondola. He (or she) is responsible for managing crews and ensuring the vessels operate safely and effectively. A gondola is lightweight but durable. Its frame is formed by Pandoran rattan cane bundled and lashed together by palm-fiber rope, creating a strong, durable structure without much weight. Each of the flotilla's gondolas is decorated with pennants, intricate patterns, and woven structures.

PULLING TOGETHER

The Wind Traders run their gondola like any Terran sailing ship—the crew manipulates the steering ropes and scrambles around in the rigging. If the gondola has to change course or tack because of a headwind, they quickly run through their paces: climbing the ratlines, even to the very top of the medusoid, where the gas pressure within the membrane is enough to support their weight. In a storm, these skilled Na'vi "batten down the hatches" at lightning speed as well. A team of eight Wind Traders works together on deck, tightening lines connected to the medusoid's sail-like vanes. Because the Na'vi don't use wheels or pulleys, they rely on their strong backs and strength of numbers. The lines are redirected through fairleads of polished shell or bone, without pulleys. Use of the "turning wheel" is prohibited under the Three Laws of *Eywa*.

FACT FILE
> The palm fiber rope has carbon spicules, which are strong and provide durable rigging for navigational purposes.
> *Ikran* belonging to the outriders or visitors may perch on the gondola's gunwales or rigging.

FLOTILLA DEFENSE

Wind Traders travel in groups for protection. They also deploy Na'vi outriders riding *ikran*, who, in addition to undertaking hunting and scouting functions, are ready to defend the flotilla from attack. Some outriders may fly ahead, as long-range scouts, ready to alert the flotilla of aerial predators, *ikran*-mounted bandits—or hazardous weather conditions. The Wind Traders have also fitted their gondolas with giant ballistae. These are armed with multiple arrows bundled together.

Paddle used to cover openings to shift pitch

PADDLE DRUMS

CAMARADERIE
Music plays a key role in Wind Trader life. They will seek out unique sounds from other clans, like Rey'tanu gourd instruments, to create new forms of expressions together.

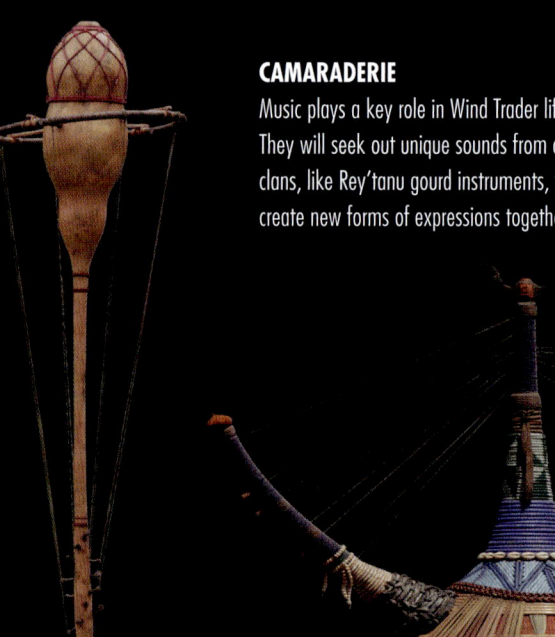

Played while standing

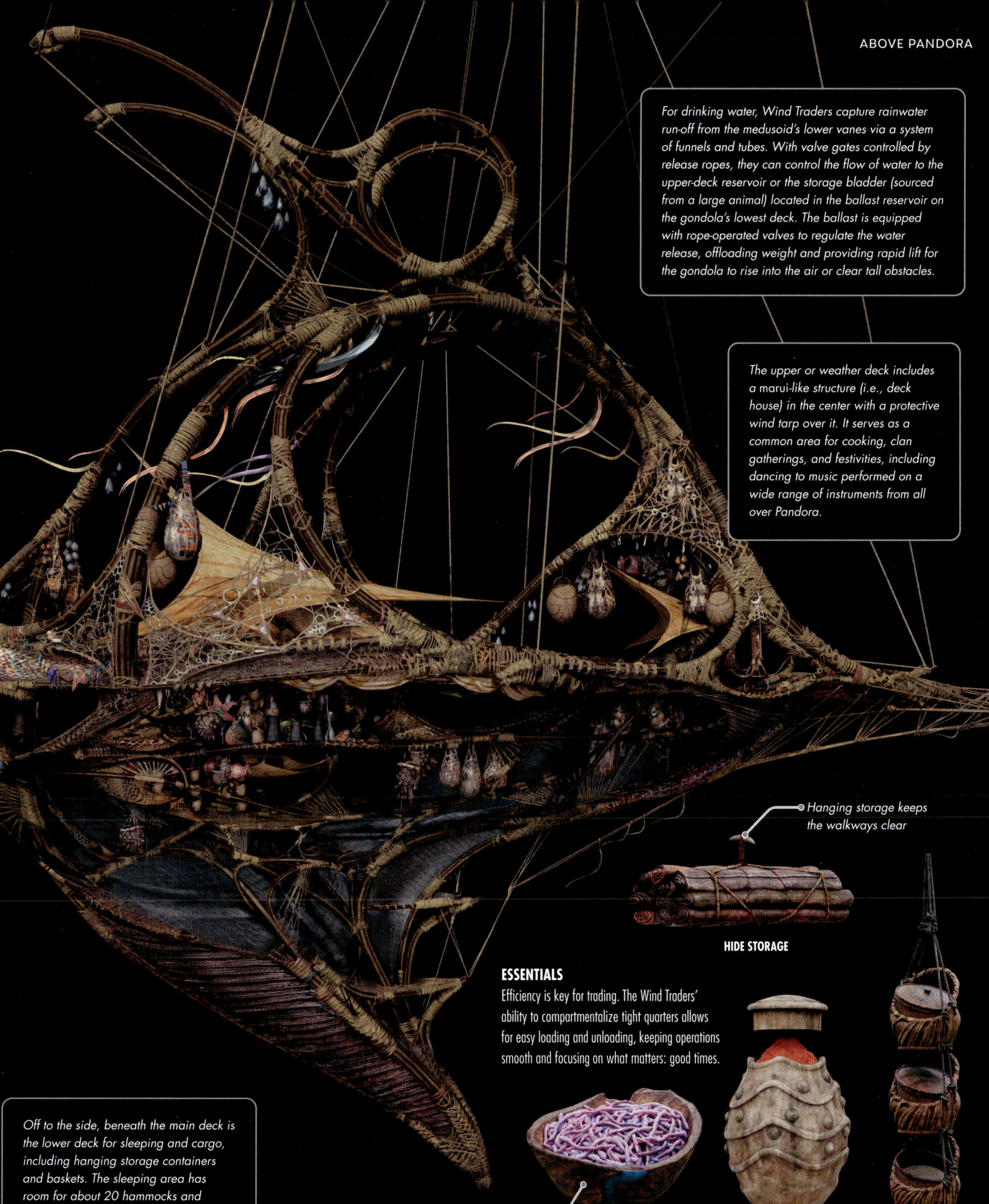

ABOVE PANDORA

For drinking water, Wind Traders capture rainwater run-off from the medusoid's lower vanes via a system of funnels and tubes. With valve gates controlled by release ropes, they can control the flow of water to the upper-deck reservoir or the storage bladder (sourced from a large animal) located in the ballast reservoir on the gondola's lowest deck. The ballast is equipped with rope-operated valves to regulate the water release, offloading weight and providing rapid lift for the gondola to rise into the air or clear tall obstacles.

The upper or weather deck includes a marui-like structure (i.e., deck house) in the center with a protective wind tarp over it. It serves as a common area for cooking, clan gatherings, and festivities, including dancing to music performed on a wide range of instruments from all over Pandora.

Hanging storage keeps the walkways clear

HIDE STORAGE

ESSENTIALS

Efficiency is key for trading. The Wind Traders' ability to compartmentalize tight quarters allows for easy loading and unloading, keeping operations smooth and focusing on what matters: good times.

Off to the side, beneath the main deck is the lower deck for sleeping and cargo, including hanging storage containers and baskets. The sleeping area has room for about 20 hammocks and provides shelter during foul weather.

Bowl reinforced by resin

WORM BOWL   **SPICE JAR**   **GRAIN BASKETS**

SAILING THE SKYWAYS

OVER THOUSANDS OF YEARS, the Wind Traders have developed a unique method of travel, harnessing medusoids to carry themselves and their cargo. A medusoid requires piloting. Its nervous system is far too primitive for *tsaheylu* (*kuru* connection), so the Wind Traders control its translucent steering vanes using braided lines. Tlalim rope is legendary for its strength, braided from a pandanus-like Pandoran plant leaf that is organically reinforced with naturally occurring carbon fiber. As the Wind Traders voyage over land and ocean, they employ a variety of rigging techniques to control elevation, direction, and speed, pulling on long reins to shift the medusoid's resplendent vanes. The medusoid may not be the swiftest ride, but it can endure for thousands of miles—long after an *ikran* gives out (an *ikran* can only fly about 75 miles (120 km) before it needs to rest, but can cover almost five times that in a normal day of riding).

STEERING A GONDOLA

To catch the wind and move forward, Wind Traders expand and fully deploy the medusoid's vanes using an intricate system of ropes. To remain stationary, the medusoid's vanes are collapsed and tucked into the sides of its body, and the gondola is typically moored to a sturdy fixed point, like a massive tree trunk or mangrove root. To gain altitude, the crew drops water from storage sacs within the gondola and the vanes are angled forward to provide lift like an airfoil. To lose altitude, they are angled back, and some gas may be expelled from the medusoid's envelope. To steer to port or starboard, one vane folds back or partially closes, to generate lateral lift, similar to a sailboat.

THE NAVIGATOR'S BOND

It is the responsibility of the navigator—riding the lead windray via *tsaheylu*—to know and sense changes in the winds along the route, and in a moment alter the altitude and direction of the flotilla accordingly. The navigator's aim is to avoid the worst of the wind and catch the best. They enter the navigator guild at an early age, and grow up learning "The Way of Air." They can literally travel with their eyes closed, as they must sometimes navigate in pitch darkness across rocky highlands where there is no bioluminescent plant cover, in case of dense overcast or storms.

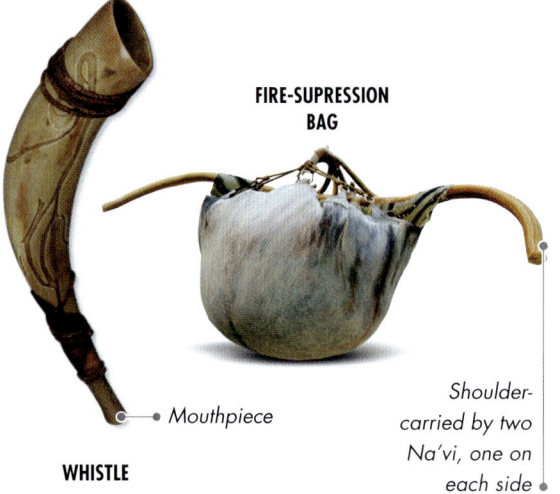

FIRE-SUPRESSION BAG

Mouthpiece

Shoulder-carried by two Na'vi, one on each side

WHISTLE

FACT FILE

> By visiting different clans, Wind Traders are able to acquire the most effective tools from each one and enhance them, thanks to their technological skills.
> A gondola's navigator mostly relies on their own knowledge of Pandora's skies and familiarity with the land below. However, they are also equipped with various tools, including maps.

CLOAK CLASP

The maps of trade winds are layered onto cloaks

POWERING A GONDOLA

Wind Traders harness large, self-propelled animals called windrays to towing bridles at the front of their gondolas. The windray pulls a gondola and its medusoid, providing forward thrust in addition to the medusoid's vanes. When the gondola is running downwind, the windray can add extra speed relative to the wind, though typically less than 15 knots of additional speed. When working cross-wind, the windray produces the necessary lateral force that a sailboat's keel would provide. With careful trimming of the medusoid's vanes, and with the windray acting as a keel, the entire system can move "faster than the wind." In mild conditions they can even tack upwind, using the medusoid's vanes in combination with thrust from the windray, but this is avoided whenever possible. Sometimes, even thousands of years of knowledge of the seasonal winds is not enough to keep the Wind Traders from encountering adverse conditions, especially in some treacherous highland crossings.

WEAPONS

ABOVE PANDORA

THE WIND TRADERS' way of life is fraught with dangers. As well as rigging knives, they carry actual weapons to ward off attacks, including giant ballistae armed with multiple arrows bundled together. With its lethal spread of projectiles being fired simultaneously, a ballista is an effective weapon against large, fast-moving aerial targets. The Wind Traders push hard against the absolute limits of technology allowed under the laws of *Eywa*.

BALLISTA

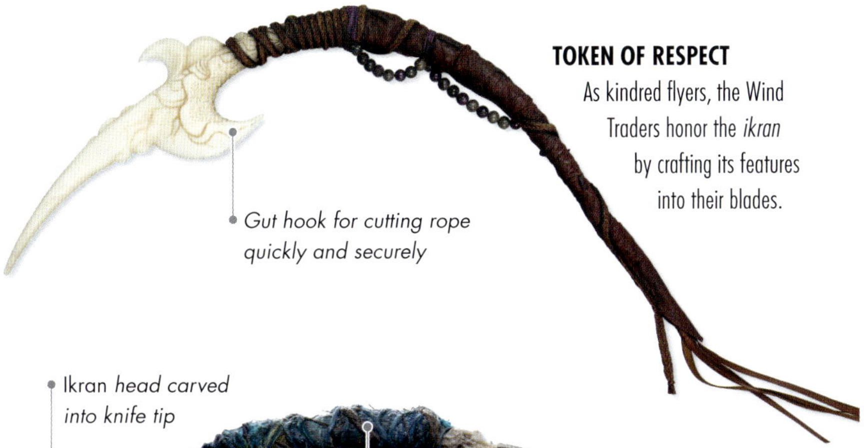

TOKEN OF RESPECT
As kindred flyers, the Wind Traders honor the *ikran* by crafting its features into their blades.

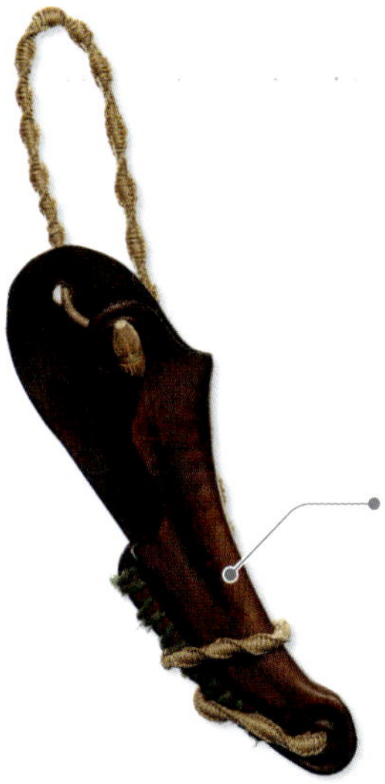

- Gut hook for cutting rope quickly and securely
- Ikran head carved into knife tip
- Color specific to rider's ikran
- Leather

KNIFE SCABBARD

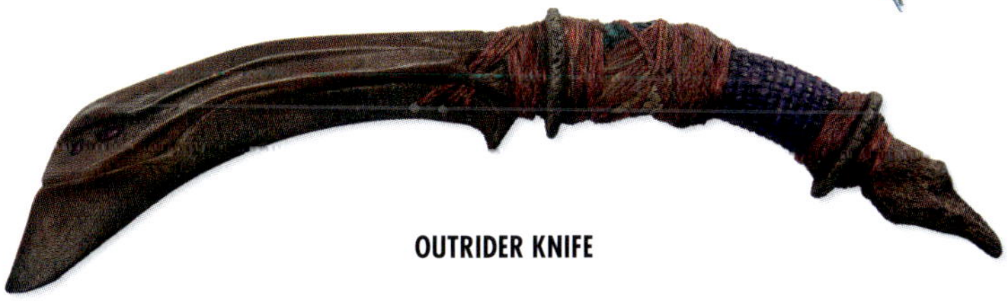

OUTRIDER KNIFE

RIGGING KNIFE

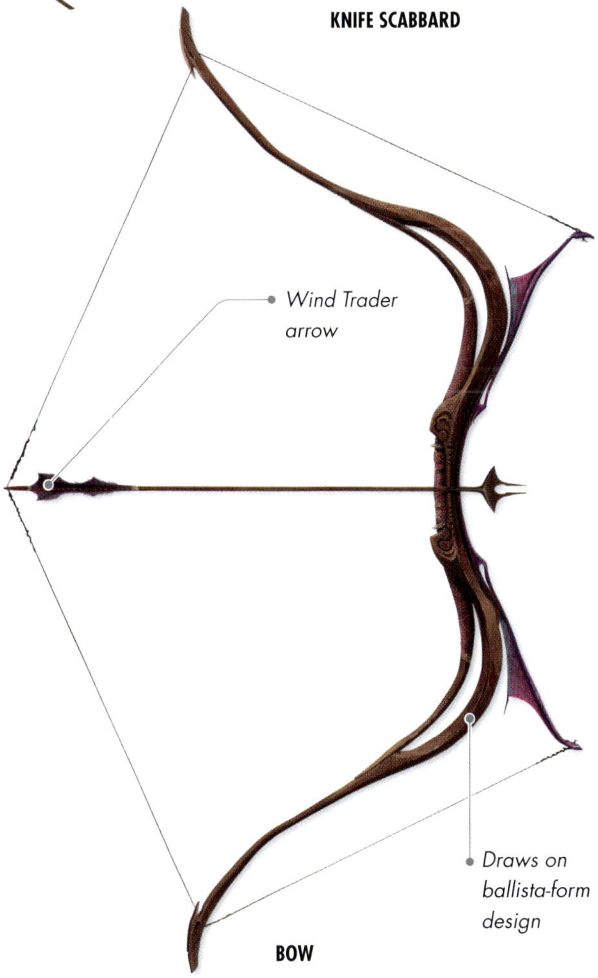

- Wind Trader arrow
- Draws on ballista-form design

BOW

SPEARS

PEYLAK

PEYLAK IS THE BRAVE AND WISE olo'eyktan of the Tlalim. As such, Peylak oversees life among the Wind Traders' gondola fleet like a ship's captain. He is responsible for managing the crews and ensuring the vessels operate safely and efficiently. Like his fellow Wind Traders, Peylak is a worldly-wise adventurer pursuing cultural exchange to find, share, and trade goods and stories.

COLLAR
- Fenestrated leaf symbolizes withstanding heavy wind

NAVIGATING UNCERTAINTY

Guided by the maxim that the wind gives and the wind takes, Peylak knows that a trader must be able to move freely. This may neccessitate staying neutral in potentially dangerous situations. When Jake as *Toruk Makto* arrives requesting safe passage for him and his family, Peylak is concerned that by bringing them aboard, the Wind Traders will show they are choosing a side in the war against the Sky People—a decision that could compel other clans to follow, and cost lives. However, he accepts Jake's offer for him and Neytiri to fly as outriders and protect the flotilla, due to reports he has heard of increased aggression from Mangkwan raiders.

SKIRT
- Displays the quality of textile the traders provide

SPEAR
- Spearhead carved from dense bone

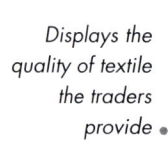

PEYLAK'S KNIFE

CUMMERBUND
- Crafted from leather, trade-wind-inspired design

PERSONAL TOTEMS
Beads and trinkets are chosen with care and story, reflecting moments from glory to humility, as any spirited adventurer can attest.

DATA FILE	
NA'VI NAME	Peylak te Tayuma Toko'itan
CLAN	Tlalim (Wind Traders)
CLAN POSITION	Olo'eyktan
BASE OF OPERATIONS	Wind Traders' gondola

ABOVE PANDORA

EXPLORER AND CAPTAIN

Peylak wears an ornate cloak signifying his status. His experience, gained through years of navigating exotic lands and surviving dangerous voyages, makes him the ideal steward of his People. Peylak possesses great knowledge of the gondola system's flight dynamics and of Pandora's wind patterns and enormously varied terrain, enabling him and his crew to quickly respond to emergencies.

- Central circle can be fitted into his wife Yu'nar's chest adornment, symbolizing their bond

- Vertebrae of an animal received as a trade from the Anurai clan

SPACER BEADS

- Shields braided kuru wrapped at the neck

NECKLACE

- Captain's cloak

LEG BAND

- Wrist wrap made of yarn from different clans

FACT FILE

› Peylak is a thoughtful leader, who prioritizes the well-being of his People.
› He is also aware of the social needs of the Wind Trader community on their long journeys, maintaining morale, and fairly resolving disputes.

MEDUSOID

DRIFTING OVER THE MOUNTAINTOPS of Pandora, the medusoid is a living bag of biogenic hydrogen gas with long tentacles, like an airborne Portuguese man-o'-war jellyfish. Its nervous system is too primitive for it to possess *kuru* or navigate itself, so this living airship floats passively in the wind, though it can vector toward potential food sources with its steering vanes and propulsive aft fins. Although it responds to stimuli, its nervous system is too primitive for centralized control, floating passively in the wind. A medusoid possesses a cluster of tentacles that hang down 478 feet (145.7 m), and they can be lethal. Medusoids use these tentacles for defense and to capture prey, raking them across an expanse of water or forest canopy.

DATA FILE

NAME Medusoid, Aerocoelenterates
NA'VI NAME *Rimo'a* (ree-moh-ah')
TAXONOMY *Medusa gigans*
HABITAT Skies over oceans, rivers, and lakes
SIZE Body: 504 ft 8 in (153.83 m) wide x 910 ft 1 in (277.39 m) high x 585 ft 2 in (178.36 m) long; Tentacles: 477 ft 11 in (145.67 m) long.

FACT FILE

> In the wild, the medusoid lives mostly over oceans and wetlands, using its tentacles to sting and capture small prey, drawing it up from the water into the mouth in the underside of the gasbag.
> The Wind Traders coax these invertebrates to fly over land, high enough so that their tentacles don't catch in the trees below.
> The medusoid may not be the swiftest ride but it has enormous lifting capacity and extraordinary powers of endurance.

TENTACULAR GRIP

A medusoid's tentacles have sensors that instantly react to the touch of an animal by curling instantly into a vise-like grip. They are also lined with electrocysts that channel a current from an organ in its bell that produces electricity. The shock can be strong enough to ward of a large predator like an *ikran*, or even kill a full-grown human. Once in the grip of these tough, rubbery appendages, it is unlikely that any creature will survive. The medusoid's tentacles then lift the prey to the creature's pulpy manubrium (mouth).

FLYING FREE

The medusoid's bell is filled with hydrogen gas, produced by digesting prey in an organ similar to a bovine rumen, a bioreactor filled with methanophilic endosymbiont bacteria. This gas allows the medusoid to float high above the land in search of feeding grounds. Its bell expels gas to descend, and dumps waste-water from trim bladders to rise. For the most part, the animal is content to drift on the wind and hunt opportunistically. Given its slow mobility, it could become easy prey for other aerial predators. However, the medusoid has little edible flesh, and the unpleasant and potentially explosive release of hydrogen gas when the bell is punctured by tooth or claw is a natural deterrent for any predator. Moreover, the powerful electric shock produced by its tentacles can stun predators and turn them into potential prey. For these reasons, a medusoid is rarely bothered. Its only consistent enemy is the great leonopteryx (*toruk*), which, if short of food, will attack the foul-tasting creature.

The Na'vi Wind Traders have learned to harness medusoid invertebrates to transport their cargo.

ABOVE PANDORA

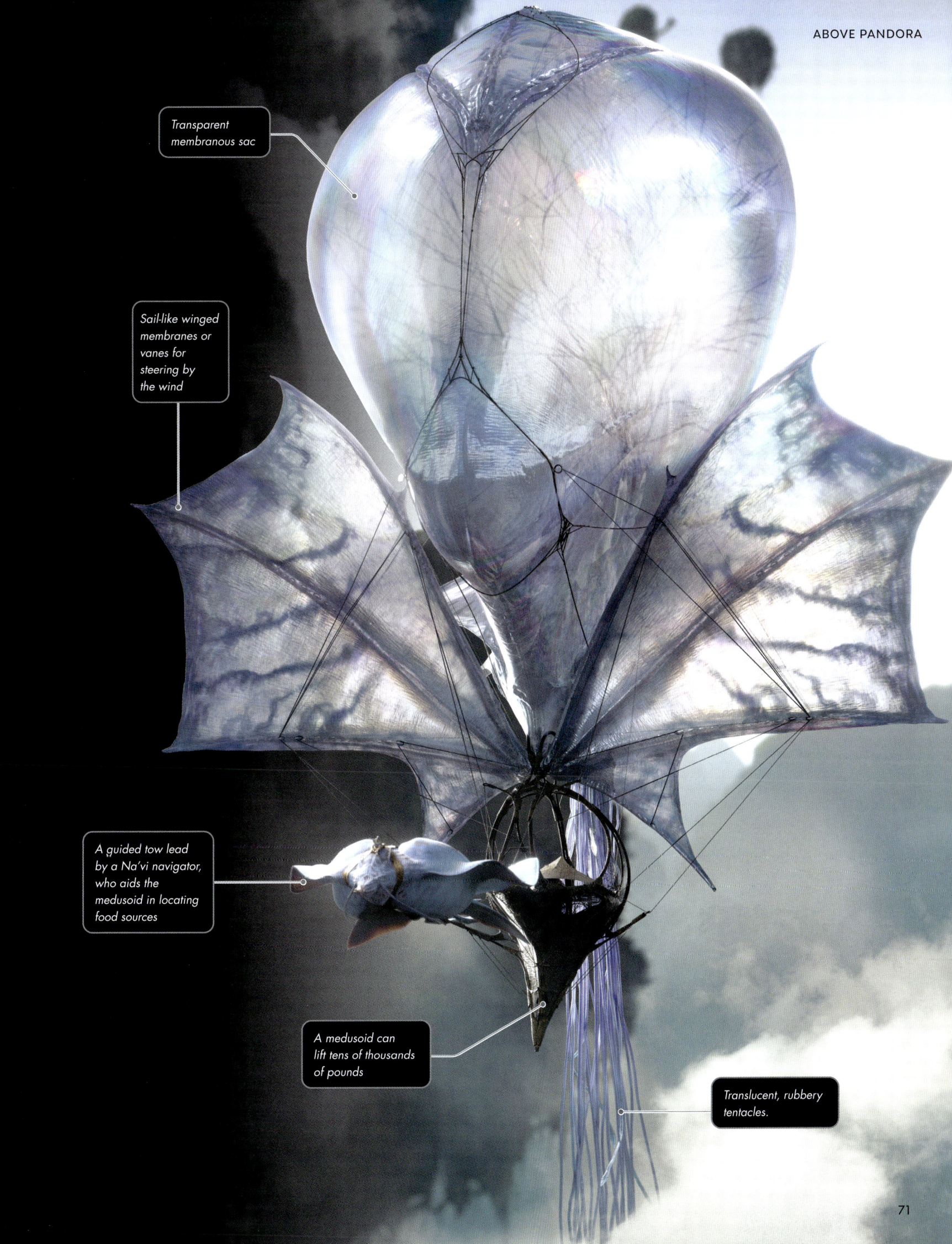

Transparent membranous sac

Sail-like winged membranes or vanes for steering by the wind

A guided tow lead by a Na'vi navigator, who aids the medusoid in locating food sources

A medusoid can lift tens of thousands of pounds

Translucent, rubbery tentacles.

WINDRAY

THE WINDRAY OR *KREYTU'UM* is a self-propelled, gas-filled animal that looks somewhat like a cross between a Terran cuttlefish and a manta ray. It is larger than a Terran blue whale and carries enough hydrogen gas to offset much of its own weight in the dense Pandoran air, though it is technically heavier than air and depends on forward motion to gain enough lift to stay airborne. However, it is such an efficient flier that it can stay airborne most of its life. The Na'vi Wind Traders harness a windray to the bow of each of their gondolas to tow medusoids, the heavy lifters, while in flight. Like a tugboat maneuvering a huge tanker, the windrays steer the whole flight system of medusoid/windray/gondola around obstacles and are used by the navigator to maintain the correct heading relative to the wind and the course, as well as providing extra propulsion. The windray's translucent body looks beautiful when backlit by the sun.

DATA FILE	
NAME	Windray
NA'VI NAME	*Kreytu'um* (kray-too-oom)
TAXONOMY	*Cognosera pastoris*
HABITAT	ocean shores, rivers, and lakes.
SIZE	Body: 124 ft 6in (37.96 m) wide; 45 ft 2 in (13.76 m) high; 225 ft 2 in (68.63 m) long; tentacles (mouth): 55 ft (16.89 m) long.

ROTATING TOW

The relationship between windrays and the navigator is symbiotic, with each animal facilitating transport while the singular Na'vi ensures their overall well-being, including knowing when and where to locate abundant food sources. When the wind is astern and favorable, the windrays are cut loose to feed in the ocean or a lake. Switching out one windray from the towing bridle for a fresh one while the convoy is underway requires agility and clever managing of lines, but the Wind Traders do it every day, seemingly without effort. At all times, the animals remain fully tacked in their woven harnesses, not to be taken off unless they become ill. Typically, a number of free windrays can be seen trailing the convoy: the spares, who are swapped in to tow the medusoids when the previous "shift" gets tired or needs to feed. Also among them are mothers nurturing young windrays. The aerial tows are raised from hatchlings to be part of the convoy and are trained to always keep up with the flotilla's formation.

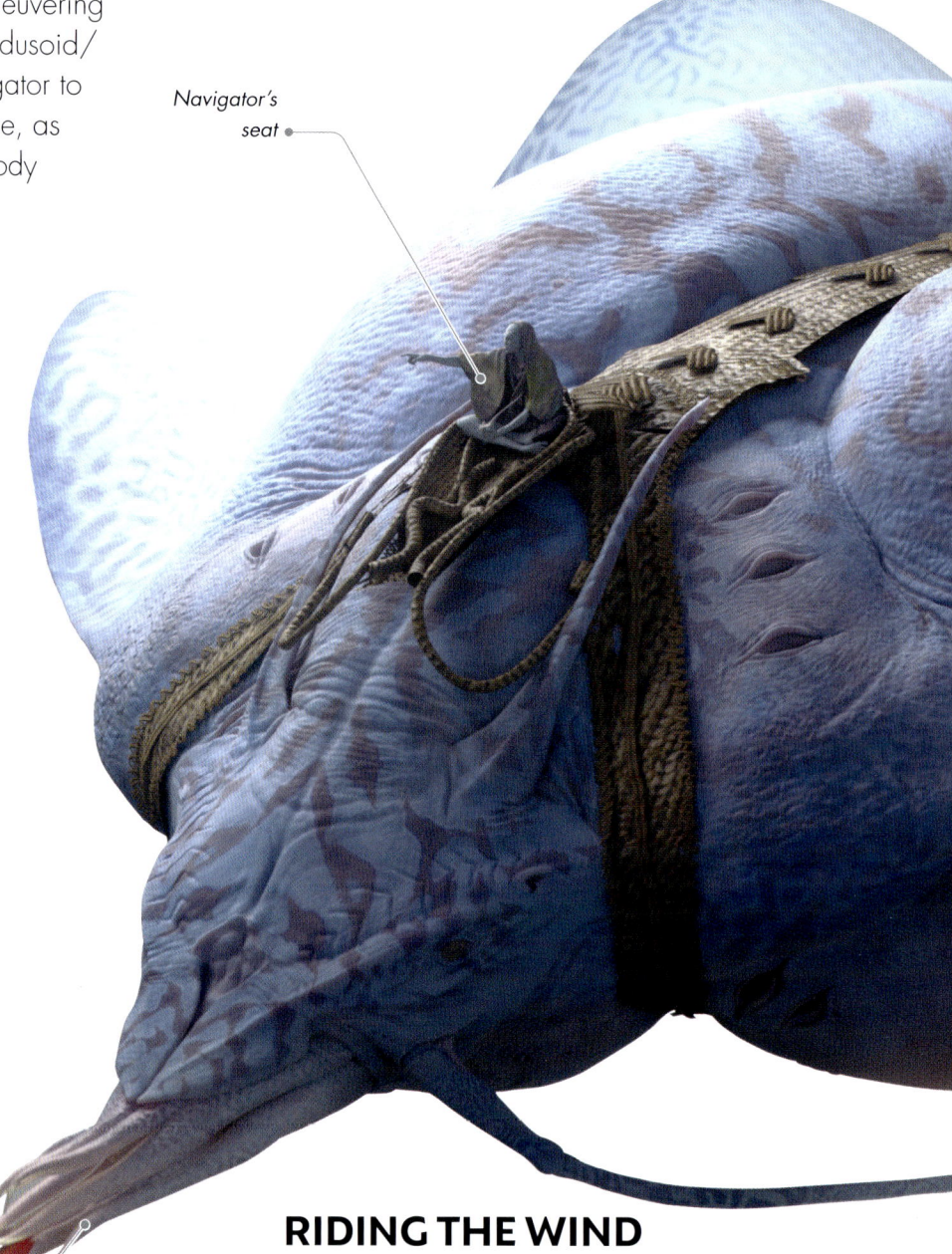

Navigator's seat

Flexible, grasping tentacles arranged around a beak with a frog-like tongue

The windray's two long whiskers trail on the water surface. Their movements attract fish. When a fish nears them, the windray shoots out its 20-foot (6.1 m) tongue and grabs it with piercing barbs. Tentacles around its mouth pull the prey to its beak.

RIDING THE WIND

The Windray's wings undulate to provide propulsion independent of the wind. Its rear fins rotate and enable it to change direction; its tail provides additional maneuverability. It also has two sets of three opercula (breathing orifices) on the ventral side to take in air, as well as on the dorsal side to expel it. The windray changes altitude through their opercula by dumping water and expelling gas to fly higher or lower.

VIEW FROM ABOVE

VIEW FROM BELOW

A tack for towing the medusoid and Wind Trader gondola upwind

Flexible membrane where hydrogen gas is stored

The navigator ensures the windray makes no sudden movements that can ripple back and knock gondola passengers off their feet

Undulating wings provide propulsion independent of the wind.

FACT FILE

> The windray's tentacles have two protective sheathes or flaps on top that contain a subcutaneous gland that secretes saliva. This lubrication reduces friction and wear between the tentacles, especially in windy conditions.
> The tentacles have a hard pallet underneath that allows them to lay at rest on long journeys, saving metabolic energy.

The lead windray navigates the Wind Trader flotilla over the Pandoran landscape.

LAND OF FIRE

IN A BLEAK, GRAY LANDSCAPE, marked by meandering dendritic channels formed by rain, wind-blown dust drifts over dunes of ash. The air is hazy, and the forest is gone except for the burned and blackened skeletons of trees half buried in the ash. A generation ago, the volcano that dominates the landscape erupted, devastating the entire region. What used to be the traditional territory of the Mangkwan People is now a wasteland, devoid of forest, devoid of food. Even parts of the nearby mangrove swamp have turned a spectral ashen white. Plants that would normally begin to regrow are unable to do so due to the recurring falls of ash.

THE MANGKWAN CLAN

DATA FILE	
NA'VI NAME	Mangkwan (mong'-kwahn)
RANGE (BIOME)	Rainforest volcanic field
BEHAVIOR	Hostile, aggressive
LANGUAGE	Na'vi dialect

THE MANGKWAN are considered an abomination by other Na'vi. Also known as the Ash People, they have forsaken the Na'vi Way of a balanced and connected lifestyle—the true path. These warlike raiders are defined by the ash from the volcanic eruption that devastated—and continues to devastate—their home. Led by their *tsahik*, Varang, they wear ash as a symbol of rejection by *Eywa*, and of owning the pain and trauma inflicted on them. They revolt against *Eywa* for her lack of intervention during the decimation of their clan, not understanding that *Eywa* has no power over natural disasters. The Mangkwan paint and style themselves to instill fear in other Na'vi and project their power. Appearing as ghostly figures in the forest, they pillage the villages of neighboring clans for food and resources, often bringing death and destruction.

FUELED BY HATE

A generation ago, the eruption of a nearby volcano displaced the Mangkwan from their Hometree. Despite returning to inhabit its ruins, time has brought no relief, as the volcano is still active. While a few individuals have fled and been taken in by other clans, as a community, the Mangkwan are prideful and have mostly remained on their land, surviving by any means necessary. For the younger Mangkwan among them, this is the only life they have ever known. To replenish their numbers they raid other clans, not just for food but for slaves, who become indoctrinated into the dark ethos of the Mangkwan. They either wear the ash, or they die.

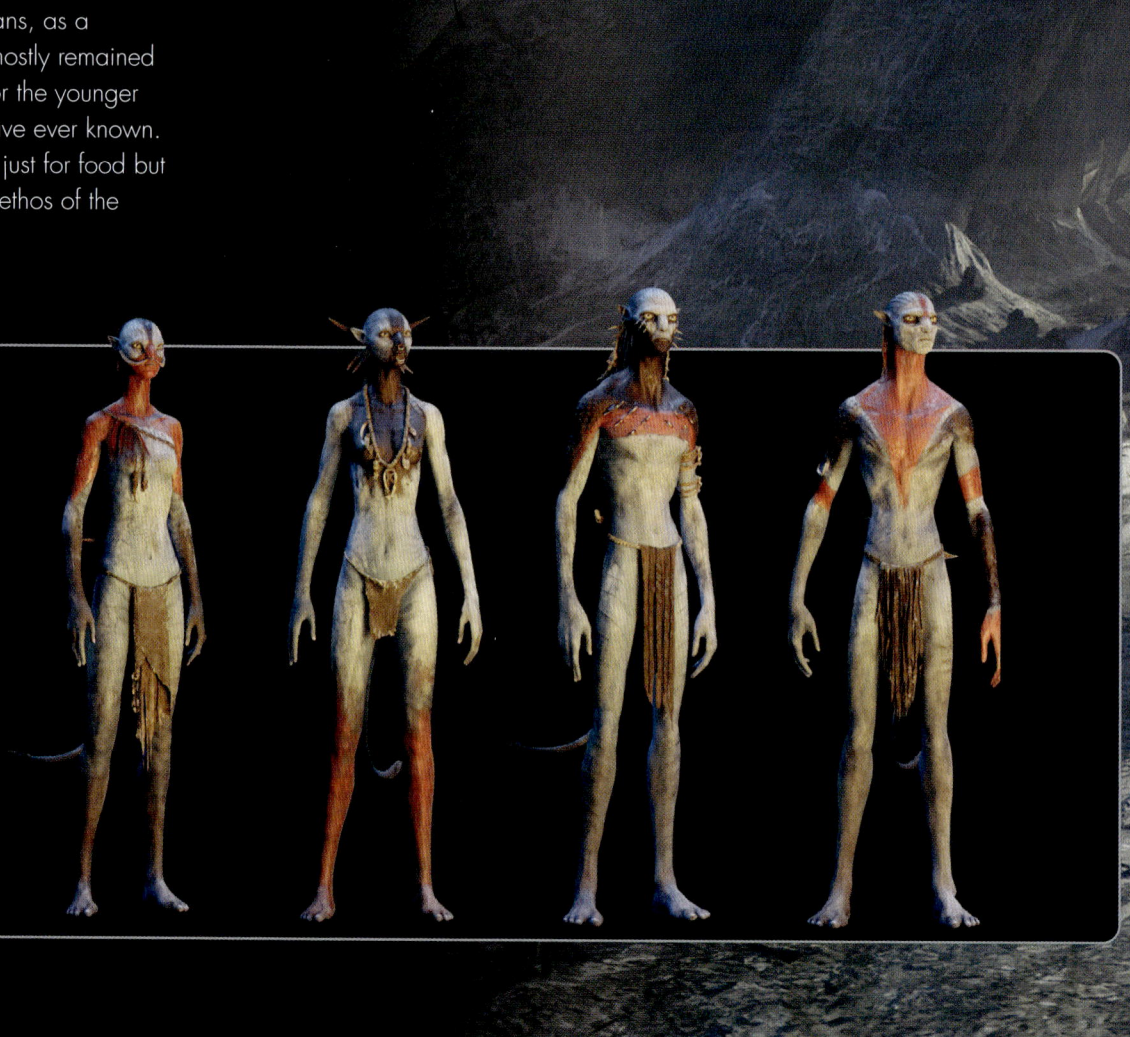

SCARS OF PRIDE

The Mangkwan cover themselves in a base of grayish white ash, with bands of red-and-black paint—the colors of the smothering ash, of blood, and of charred wood—wearing their pain symbolically. The clan also applies piercings and scarification to their bodies, inflicting violence on themselves like the violence that created their down-twisted psychology. They pride themselves on their ability to endure pain. By evoking fear in other clans, they find strength and power, as well as notoriety in the name given to them: the Ash People.

LAND OF FIRE

Ikran *roost on the ridges and broken root columns of the Mangkwan Hometree*

FALLEN HOMETREE

Time has compacted the ash and hardened it into dense layers of tuff, which in certain areas has built up 40 feet (12 m) above the original ground level. It covers the base of the Mangkwan clan's burned-out Hometree, where broken root columns form a jagged crown, reaching toward the sky in a radial pattern. The massive spiral trunk collapsed sideways as the base columns burned, and now lies sprawled out across the landscape. The tree's mighty branches, once forming a canopy almost a thousand feet across, now rear against the sky like clawed hands, blackened and skeletal. The near end of the fallen trunk towers ominously behind the village, a blackened maw.

SPREADING DESTRUCTION

Wherever the Mangkwan go, they spread fire and ash. After they raid a village, they burn it to the ground, evoking the destruction of their ancestral Hometree. There is a ritual element of self-conscious pageantry to their actions—it is an orchestrated spectacle of brutality. The Mangkwan keenly comprehend the psychological impact of their actions on those they wish to conquer. It is a calculated projection of power ultimately designed to subjugate them.

ASH VILLAGE

THE MANGKWAN'S VILLAGE is the base from which the clan raids. It is nested in the center of their Hometree ruins. The designs of their yurts, while functional and practical, display a sinister version of Na'vi artistic symmetry. The Mangkwan aesthetic blends brutality and theatrics, with disturbing displays of skulls, bones, and the severed *kuru* of other Na'vi. They have no qualms about cutting down trees to build their yurts, defying *Eywa*'s precepts to balance the Pandoran ecosystem. The clan further emphasizes its rejection of *Eywa* by the excessive killing of animals, for whom they do not offer the Prayer for the Dead, or any ritual blessing to signify the Great Balance.

MANGKWAN YURT

Though crude in appearance, the Mangkwan yurt is a rigid dwelling that is durable for individual or family units. Despite the effort of building and maintaining a yurt, most Mangkwan, however, still have the residual memory that their Hometree is sheltering them.

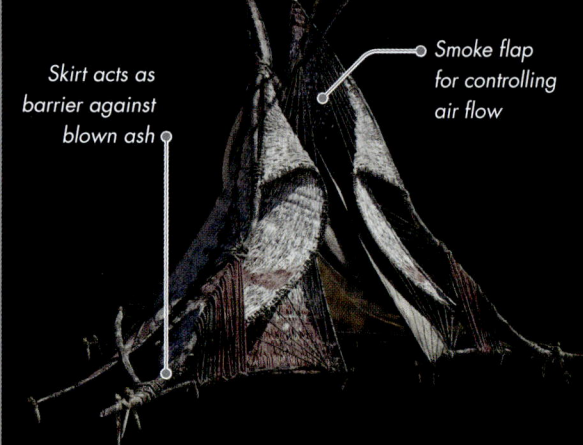

Skirt acts as barrier against blown ash

Smoke flap for controlling air flow

VILLAGE TOTEMS

Two totems stand at the heart of the village. Each one has a demonic face with predatory horns on the side of its head. They are meant to strike fear in the Na'vi and inspire blind obedience in the Mangkwan.

RIKU

The strongest Mangkwan fighter, Riku battles with a spear fashioned to pierce an enemy's heart, allowing him to stare them down as they expire. Varang's right hand, he sacrificed his eye for her while raiding a village that wouldn't surrender quietly. The anger Riku harbors from a prior surprise attack fuels him to keep his wits about him, vowing never to let anyone have the advantage again. Relentless and ruthless, he never lets his guard down.

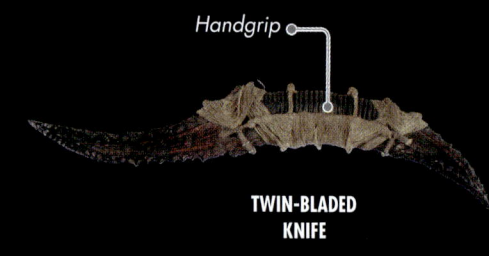

Handgrip

TWIN-BLADED KNIFE

DATA FILE

FULL NA'VI NAME Riku (Ree'-koo)

CLAN Mangkwan

CLAN POSITION Warrior, alpha male, under Varang

BASE Mangkwan village

Meat is chopped and carried on a rack to a fire pit for cooking.

LAND OF FIRE

The active volcano is an ever-present sight.

Hanging totem

ASH VILLAGE LIFE

THE MANGKWAN TAKE perverse pride in the tough conditions they live in, believing that their severe lifestyle defines their identity and emphasizes their superiority over all other clans. They are convinced that no other clan on Pandora would have the indomitable spirit to survive—and thrive—in their chosen volcanic wasteland.

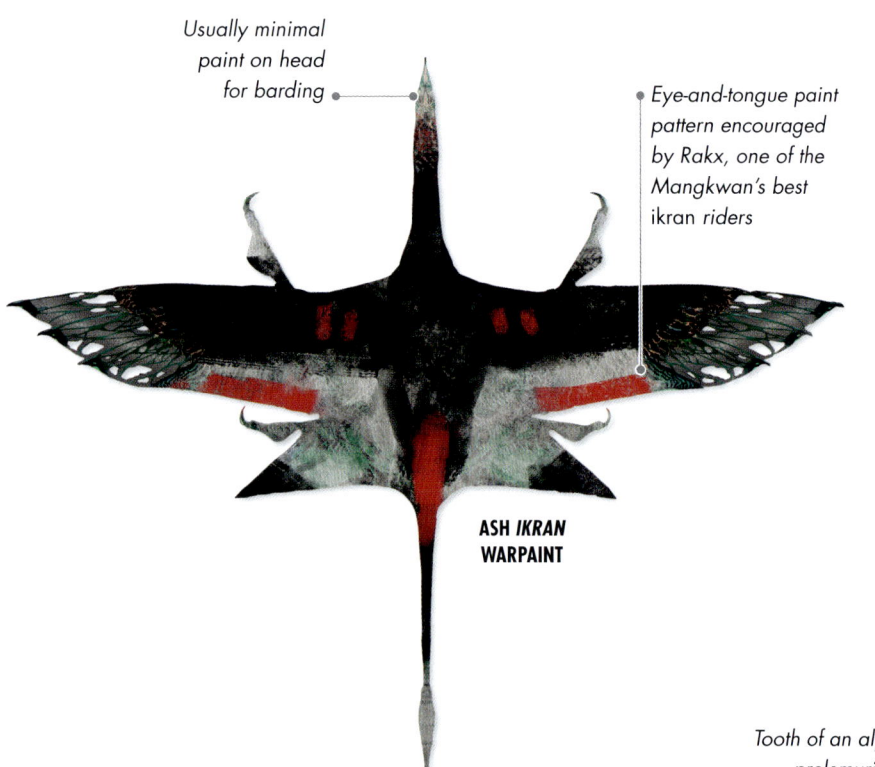

- Usually minimal paint on head for barding
- Eye-and-tongue paint pattern encouraged by Rakx, one of the Mangkwan's best ikran riders
- Dive-bomber pattern by a sacrificial Na'vi warrior

ASH IKRAN WARPAINT

ASH IKRAN WARPAINT

HUNTING

Small teams of Mangkwan scouts venture into the distant woods to hunt wildlife with bows, arrows, and knives. Unlike all other Na'vi, the Mangkwan prefer to avoid a quick kill, and instead, incapacitate the animal and leave it suffering until it is returned to the village. This is done to prevent the meat from spoiling on the long journey home, but also fits their mindset. They reduce their own feelings of suffering by inducing it in others, whether animal or Na'vi. Each such act is an utter denunciation of *Eywa*'s ethos of the Great Balance, which is respectful of all life, and of the connections between all living beings.

COOKING AND EATING

Mangkwan hunt and kill their food as individuals, only sharing with those who help in the kill. Their diet consists largely of meat as a source of calories, since fruits spoil before they can be transported into their wasteland stronghold, and they don't have the patience or the soil for growing plots of grains or vegetables. Typically, the Mangkwan grill and eat kills over an open fire.

- Skull cup is referred to by some Mangkwan as Artsut

BOWLS

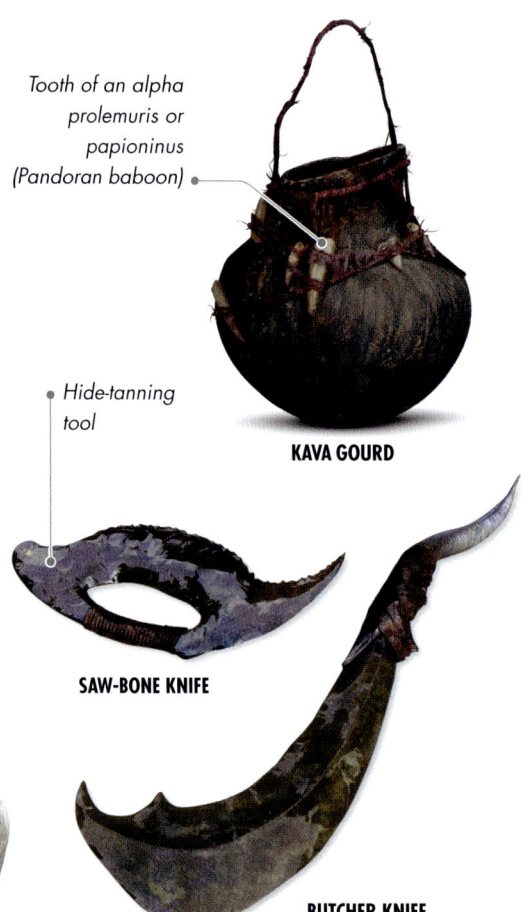

- Tooth of an alpha prolemuris or papioninus (Pandoran baboon)
- Hide-tanning tool

KAVA GOURD

SAW-BONE KNIFE

BUTCHER KNIFE

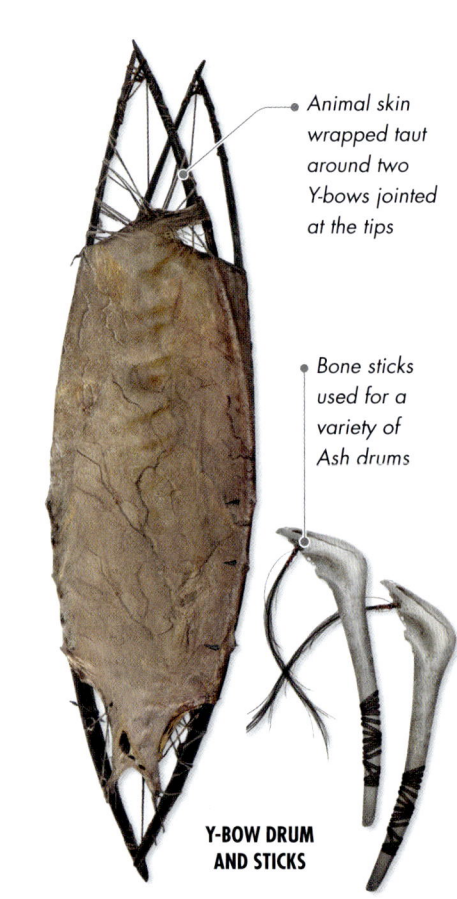

- Animal skin wrapped taut around two Y-bows jointed at the tips
- Bone sticks used for a variety of Ash drums

Y-BOW DRUM AND STICKS

GARMENTS

What little clothing the Mangkwan wear is made from dried animal hide. Most pieces are intentionally designed to inflict pain upon the wearer. They tightly bind their biceps, thighs, and torso with sturdy leather bands. Strong female Mangkwan apply the same tight binds across their breasts to deny the natural Na'vi form intended by *Eywa*.

Hide stretched across a ridged surface to be made pliable

HIDE-SOFTENING FRAME

DIREHORSE HIDE

NOSE PIERCING
The Mangkwan piercings are self-inflicted; they wield sharp blades and cauterize them with red-hot metal, fusing flesh with fire.

LOINCLOTH

Repurposed metal strips

CHOKER

CHEST PIECE

STANDARD WARRIOR GARB

LOINCLOTH WITH ORNAMENTAL METAL

NECKLACE

BONE WRIST WRAP

EARRING

ARM PIERCING

MANGKWAN WEAPONS

TERRIFYING TALES of Na'vi being attacked by the Ash People establish the Mangkwan's reputation as the most feared clan on Pandora. Mangkwan combat strategies are brutal, and they possess more battle experience and lethal weaponry than any other clan. Those lucky enough to escape or survive tell stories so disturbing that at first other Na'vi believe them to be wildly exaggerated. However, every story is soon proven by open wounds and festering burns—or worse, brutally hacked *kuru*, leaving victims dead in the eyes of *Eywa*. Mangkwan warriors also force *tsaheylu* with their dying enemies so that they not only see but feel life drain from their bodies.

COMBAT READY
Among other Mangkwan primed with a tested assortment of deadly weapons, a warrior is positioned to strike with a Y-bow and arrow.

TO THE DEATH
The Ash People's fanaticism knows no bounds. Mangkwan warriors willingly sacrifice themselves, sometimes by self-immolation, so their family will gain status. To bring down a Wind Trader gondola, for example, a Mangkwan warrior will set themself on fire and plunge in a vertical dive, using the sharply pointed helmet of their *ikran* to pierce the medusoid's membrane, igniting the hydrogen gas within. The resulting inferno will quickly kill the medusoid and plunge the gondola to the ground, where it can be pillaged.

FLENSING BLADE

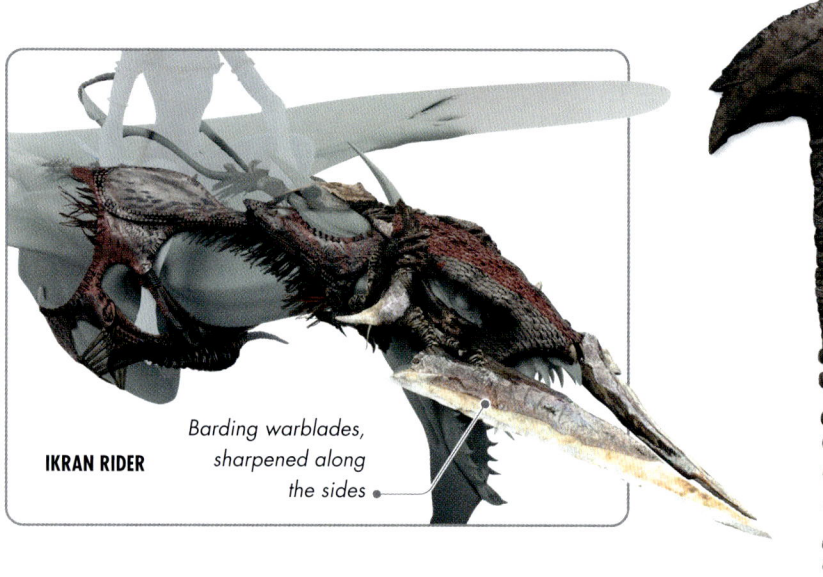

IKRAN RIDER

Barding warblades, sharpened along the sides

Flensing blade made of dark stained bone used to puncture and rip oil bag

Oil bag used by warriors to light themselves on fire

Burning embers to light a flaming arrow

Dried animal hide cover

BOLAS
Mangkwan bolas are constructed from tightly woven Na'vi hair rope around resinous seedpods. They are swung above the head and flung toward the target. The bolas wrap around the victim's legs, immobilizing them.

Heavy seedpods

LAND OF FIRE

BOWS

While the traditional hunting bow is a part of their arsenal, the Mangkwan also deploy the X-bow and Y-bow. With the bows' two upper limbs and either one or two lower limbs, warriors can fire at long range with incredible accuracy. Additionally, they use the vertices of the upper limbs to restrain and lead captives by the neck with ease. The more powerful X-bow can fold like a traditional bow for easy storage, while the slimmer Y-bow offers better maneuverability. Unlike other clans that assign meaning to their bows using ceremonial wood, Mangkwan bows are constructed from trees intentionally cut down. Arrows are fashioned similarly, with arrowheads made from carved stones or metal.

Red-dyed fletching

Grooves lock the bow in an X formation

Y-BOW **BOW** **X-BOW** **ARROWS**

KNIVES

More care is taken over the handle. This is not for fashion, but function. Wound leather and fabric around the handle provide a secure grip. And unlike other clans, the Mangkwan do not use knife sheaths. Instead, knives are tucked into their waistbands, as they're unfazed by any injuries that might occur.

Stained black bone handle

Handle fashioned from an animal horn

Salvaged RDA metal

Red obsidian

MELEE WEAPONS

Mangkwan spears and halberds are crafted in the same style as their knives with minimum focus on fashion and maximum focus on function. Constructed from bone, wood, and metal, Mangkwan weapons are heavy, but warriors train to leverage this to their advantage, using them to bludgeon enemies into submission.

CLEAVER **DOUBLE EDGE** **SPEAR** **HALBERD**

VARANG

THE FORMIDABLE YOUNG *tsahik* of the Mangkwan is a ruthless sorceress who has turned traditional *tsahik* knowledge of the herbal plant and spirit realms into a dark art of poison and curses. As the first of the "Fallen Na'vi," Varang has convinced her clan to forsake *Eywa* and the Na'vi Way because of *Eywa*'s lack of intervention in the volcanic eruption that devastated their home. Driven by revenge and lust for power, she leads the Mangkwan's raids on other clans, seeking to ensure the Ash People's survival and establish them as the most feared clan on Pandora.

DATA FILE
NA'VI NAME *Varang* (other names unknown)
CLAN Mangkwan
CLAN POSITION *Tsahik*
BASE Mangkwan Hometree Ruins

Lightweight, made of bone, leather, metal, and wire

EARRINGS

Black obsidian

ARMBAND

A REMORSELESS RISE

Varang is one of the few surviving members of the Mangkwan who witnessed first-hand the volcanic upheaval that led to the destruction of their Hometree and the death of her mother, the clan's *tsahik*. When she came of age, she took her mother's place as *tsahik*, displacing her older sister, who was *tsahik*-in-waiting. At age 15, Varang seized control of the clan, poisoning her *olo'eyktan* father, whom she considered a weak leader blinded by fear. She has been running the clan ever since, as their fierce messiah, their savior, their Mother.

BLADED WEAPONRY
Sharp and lethal, Varang's buugeng crystal blades are often wielded in combat and used to sever the *kuru* of Na'vi, but they are also spun during fire dances to coax the flames and invoke the Mangkwan spirit.

Headress marks Varang's standing among her clan

Leather binding for agility in combat

Raised scarification

LAND OF FIRE

Varang draws strength and power from the essence of fire.

DARK ARTS

For her flagrant transgressions against the Na'vi Way, Varang is despised by all other Na'vi *tsahiks*. None of Varang's skills are true sorcery; they are rooted in ethno-botany, psychosomatic ritual, hypnosis and hallucinogenic medicine. She uses her herbal knowledge both to terrorize and subdue other clans and also to make her People utterly fearless and crazed with aggression—heedless of pain and emboldened as warriors. Varang has few pleasures greater than imagining *Eywa* and her followers suffering. She takes joy in administering pain to other Na'vi she considers weak, which in turn makes her feel strong, and no longer the terrified child she was during the dark years when volcanic fire and ash decimated her People.

EYE TATTOO

BATTLE CLOAK AND HEADDRESS

- Collar made from animal vertebrae with protruding spines
- Quills

TSAHÌK NECKLACE

- Gemstone color and shape evoke fire and Varang's eye tattoo
- Spiraled metal

BLOWPIPE AND DUST POUCH

- The only surviving item from the previous *tsahìk*

- Thanator hide shields her weapon arm and sets her apart visually—a mark of status among warriors
- Blade catcher for melee fighting, can also serve as a gut hook to cut open skin
- Sharp points shaped through pressure flaking with a viperwolf tooth

ARM GAUNTLET

VARANG'S BARBED KNIFE
Crafted from obsidian taken from the outer slopes of the volcano, an established Mangkwan ritual.

FACT FILE

> Varang is a born strategist, leader, and fearsome fighter. If she cannot control you, she must destroy you.

> Her favorite method of controlling others is to connect her *kuru* to another Na'vi's—as if achieving *tsaheylu* with an animal. This inflicts excruciating agony, and allows Varang to enjoy her prisoner's suffering first-hand.

VARANG'S YURT

At the end of the rows of yurts in the Ash Village stands the largest one of all. This belongs to Varang. Her lavish yurt showcases her importance and influence, featuring art totems, woven items, and rare fabrics raided from other villages. It also contains a brazier for rituals and black sorcery, as well as hooks that serve a number of arcane purposes—from ritual torture to her own violent spiritual cleansing, a way of embracing pain and preparing for battle. Most notable are the Na'vi skulls and *kuru* arranged throughout. These are displays of conquest, belonging to rival clan leaders and warriors. Oftentimes they are brought to her as gifts by her best fighters. The abundance of artifacts inside Varang's yurt epitomizes her power, and she's far from done building upon them.

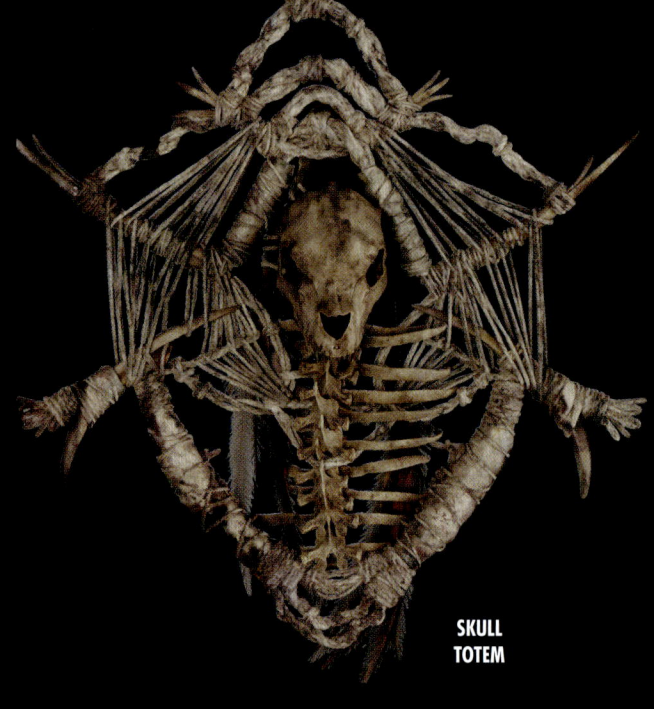

SKULL TOTEM

Varang's yurt stands at the far end of the village thoroughfare, next to the Mangkwan war drum.

RUGGED ABODE

The materials of Varang's yurt consist of animal hide, jute, and flexible rattan-like strips for the side tarps, with woven flax covering the interior floor. The roof weave is made of natural plant fibers from the closest forest entwined into rope patterns. Ventilation runs along the top and the sides to let smoke out, specifically for Varang's fire-based practices. Like all yurts in the village, the overall structure is supported by bamboo and tree branches.

BEADED CURTAIN
A ritual screen at the entrance marks the threshold of Varang's domain.

FIRE PIT

LAND OF FIRE

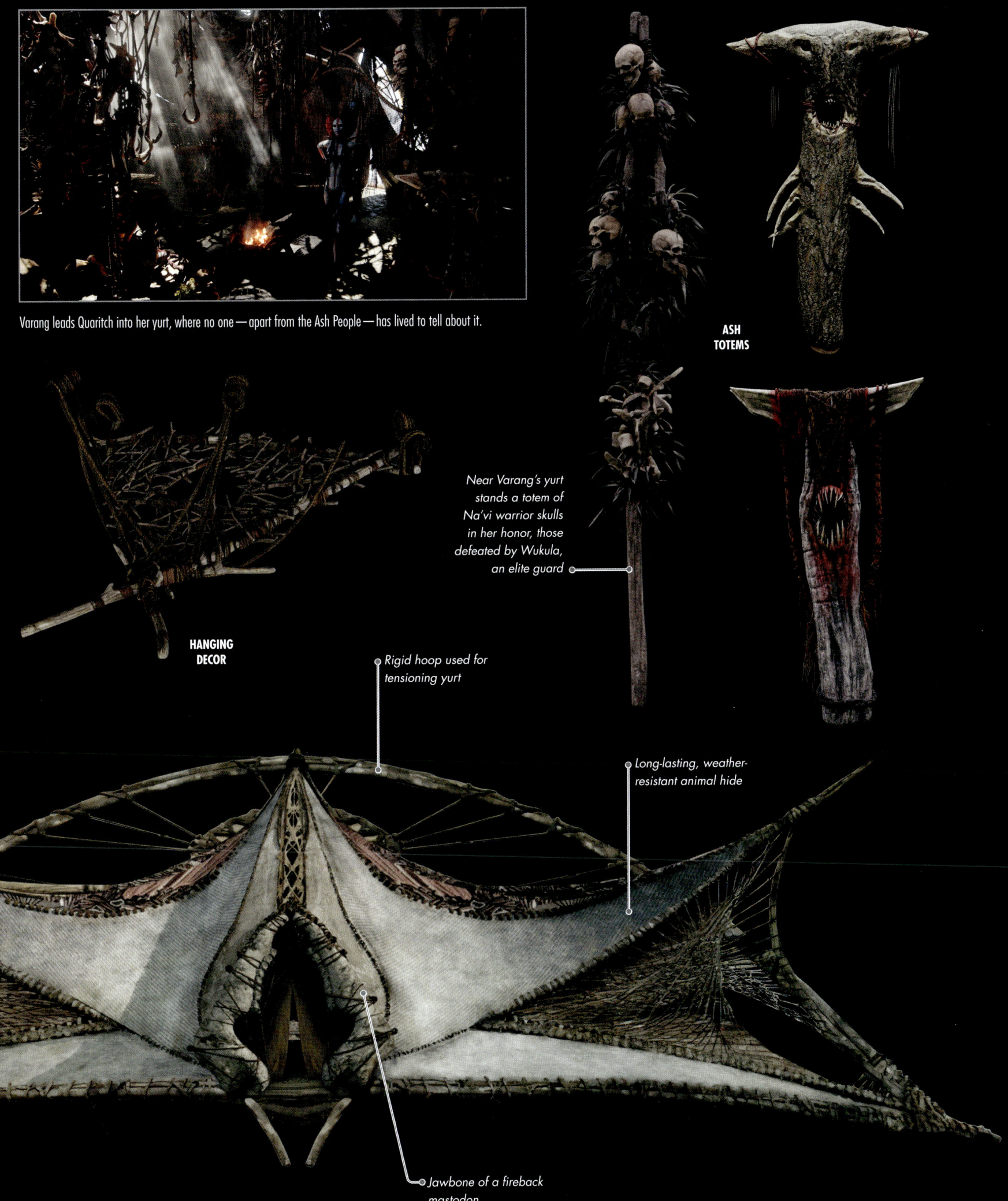

Varang leads Quaritch into her yurt, where no one—apart from the Ash People—has lived to tell about it.

ASH TOTEMS

Near Varang's yurt stands a totem of Na'vi warrior skulls in her honor, those defeated by Wukula, an elite guard

HANGING DECOR

Rigid hoop used for tensioning yurt

Long-lasting, weather-resistant animal hide

Jawbone of a fireback mastodon

NIGHTWRAITH

> **DATA FILE**
> **NAME** Nightwraith
> **NA'VI NAME** Ska'avum
> **TAXONOMY** Polydactylus volans
> **HABITAT** Rainforest volcanic field
> **ANATOMY** Aerial predator body type with four sets of ten vanes for fine flight control; head features a prominent crest.

VARANG CEMENTED her image of power by choosing as her personal mount an apex predator rarely tamed by a Na'vi rider—the nightwraith. When she returned one day astride this mount, she instantly became a living legend among her People and her reputation spread rapidly within the region. A four-winged tetrapteron, the nightwraith is an elegant and fearsome predator. Its four sets of ten vanes splay across the tips of its fore and aft pairs of wings, like folding fans generating lift and providing fine control in flight for precise attacks, even outmaneuvering the *ikran*. Additionally, its split tail provides a significant advantage to its acrobatics by reducing air resistance. With razor-sharp teeth, thrashing claws, and piercing crest bone, the nightwraith is a "ballet of death" to everything in its path.

COMMON TRAITS
The nightwraith's cranial structure aligns with that of the tetrapteron and stingbat, suggesting a shared taxonomic origin. Both smaller species feed independently of one another, but can swarm together opportunistically to target larger prey.

A MYSTERIOUS SPECIES

The tetrapteron is understood to be a complex of closely related species across various environments, exhibiting physical variations while sharing a common phylogenetic origin. Whether the Great Western tetrapteron with its bifurcated beak or the Wetland's Luna tetrapteron with *ikran*-like transparent vanes, they all share an evolutionary history. The nightwraith is a distant branch of the tetrapteron family tree. Scientists theorize that, given its uncharacteristically large size and white skin, it may be a hybrid of an unspecified flying species with an inherited condition of albinism. The enigmatic nightwraith has piqued scientific interest, raising questions about how the term "species" is defined on Pandora.

Varang targets a Wind Trader gondola on her deadly mount, poised to seize its cargo.

LAND OF FIRE

BIRD OF PREY

Offensive tactics for the nightwraith involve stabbing with its casque, targeting the exposed operculum of another animal, or striking with its hind claws like an Earth hawk or eagle. Both methods are deadly and, as a result, *ikran* do not usually challenge this larger raptor. The nightwraith's prey consists of both aerial and land fauna, including megafauna like the sturmbeest. It uses the same hunting technique as the Na'vi: isolating an animal from its herd. The nightwraith employs the sensory whiskers or barbels around its mouth to track smaller prey among trees, then uses its casque to root them out.

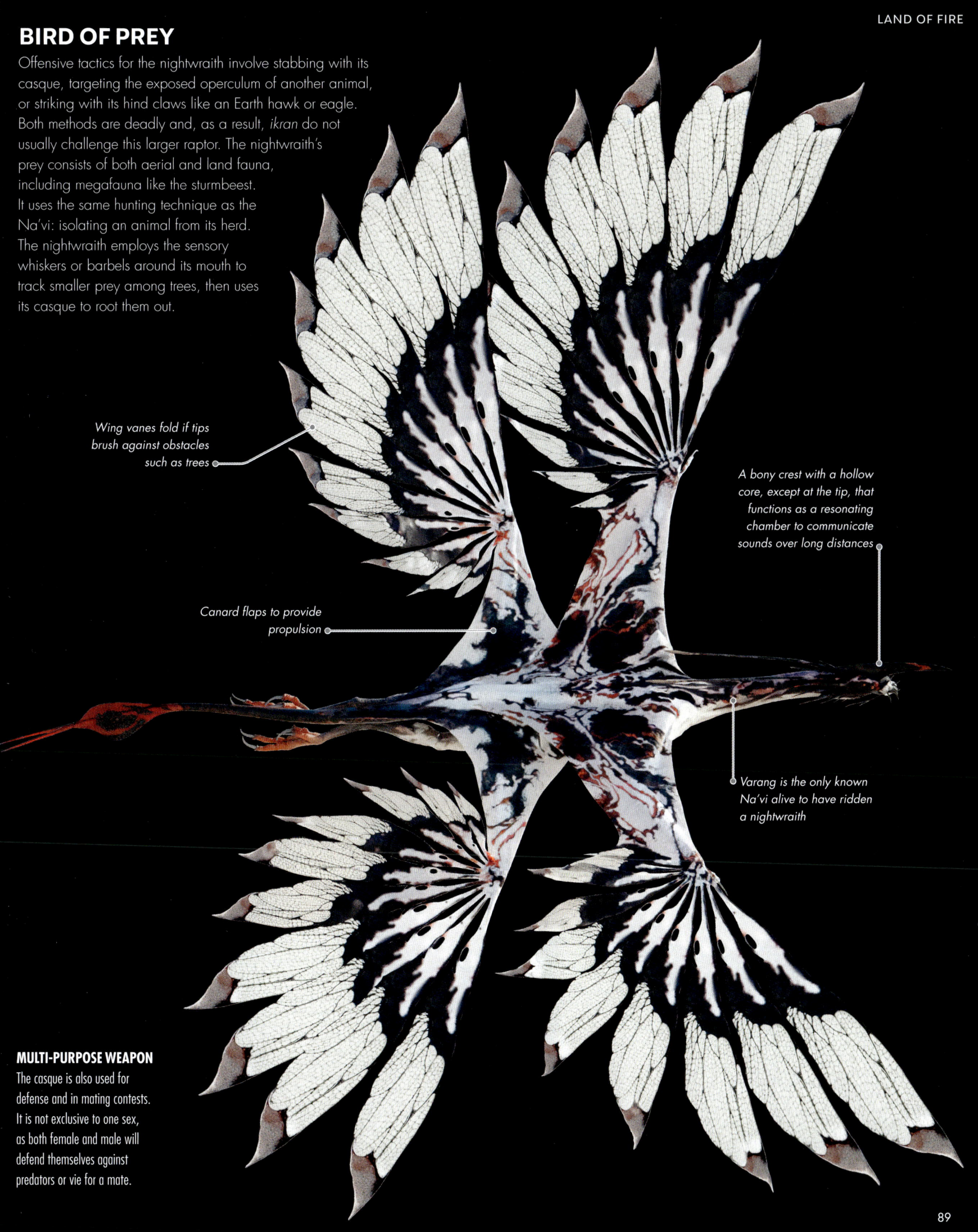

Wing vanes fold if tips brush against obstacles such as trees

A bony crest with a hollow core, except at the tip, that functions as a resonating chamber to communicate sounds over long distances

Canard flaps to provide propulsion

Varang is the only known Na'vi alive to have ridden a nightwraith

MULTI-PURPOSE WEAPON

The casque is also used for defense and in mating contests. It is not exclusive to one sex, as both female and male will defend themselves against predators or vie for a mate.

SWAMPLANDS

RAINFOREST SWAMPS on Pandora are vast wetlands usually associated with river deltas, and often seasonal, expanding during monsoon seasons of extreme rainfall. Some wetland areas remain flooded all year with stagnant water and scattered with dead trees and logs. This saturated condition reduces oxygen, traps carbon dioxide, and promotes the growth of parasitic fungi that leach nutrients. Yet the ecosystem harbors forms of life that thrive in wet areas. Pandora's swamps are home to centipedes, like the giant rivernox and its smaller relative, the neoteni, as well as lush vegetation. These species play a role in the slow recovery of the environment by feeding on decomposing material. What may at first appear a threatening atmosphere is actually contributing to the continual rejuvenation of the rainforest.

SWAMP FAUNA AND FLORA

ANIMALS SIMILAR to Earth's mangrove crabs and centipedes, flies, and mosquitoes thrive in the humid conditions of Pandora's swamps. Though some creatures—as well as some plants—are potentially life-threatening to Na'vi and humans, these species play a role in the slow recovery of the environment by feeding on decay and recycling nutrients back into the ecosystem.

Size comparison of rivernox and neoteni centipedes.

A neoteni centipede crawls along a branch above the swamp water in search of prey.

RIVERNOX CENTIPEDE

The rivernox is a giant aquatic centipede found in wetland habitats. It has a large pair of mandibles used for capturing prey and defense. It primarily feeds at night on small fish and arthropods like crabs, however, like a Terran crocodile, it is known to ambush larger prey on the banks of the swamp, including Na'vi. The cerci at the end of its abdomen has two lateral extensions that are used for grasping, for defense, and for mating. These extensions also serve as visual deterrents for would-be predators. The centipede's mandibles are highly venomous, and if that's not enough, it can spray a foul odor from glands at the base of its cerci to ward off predators. Removing its scent requires significant effort.

- *Claw-shaped mandibles*
- *More than 100 legs of various sizes*
- *Abdomen lined with small terminal legs for detecting vibrations in the water*
- *Pincer-like cerci*

DATA FILE

NAME Rivernox Centipede

NA'VI NAME Pxayknam Onvä'

TAXONOMY Aquapeda trebex

HABITAT Rivers, lakes, and swamps.

ANATOMY Multi-segmented and legged arthropod with a large pair of mandibles and a cerci (terminal body segment) with two lateral extensions.

SIZE Adults range from 10 to over 16 ft (3 to over 5 m) in length.

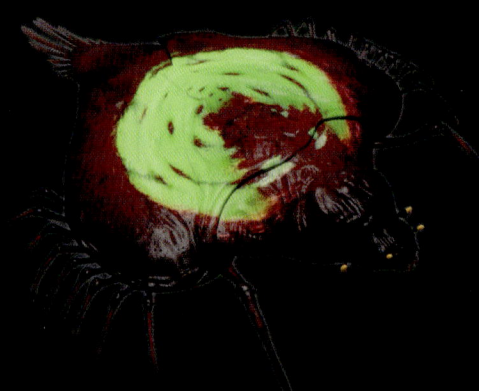

CUIRASS MUD CRAB

The cuirass mud crab feeds on a variety of foods, including algae, invertebrates, mollusks, and small fish, breaking down organic matter for fungi. Despite its hard shell and spiny tail, centipedes feed on them. Mud crabs tend to gather together in colonies for protection on tree branches and trunks.

SWAMPLANDS

NEOTENI CENTIPEDE

The neoteni centipede, or neotenipede for short, lives in rivers, lakes, and swamps coexisting with the larger rivernox centipede. Theirs is a symbiotic relationship whereby the smaller centipede attracts hungry fish, enabling the larger one to seize them. As a result, the neotenipede is able to securely feed on abundant invertebrates, such as small insects and arthropods without significant competition. It retains its larval form into adulthood, with scales extending over its head and two antennae situated between two sets of venomous claws. These are fatal to its tiny prey and also serve as a defense. For larger animals and Na'vi, they cause a stinging pain, but are not generally fatal.

The flying invertebrate forms part of the neotenipede's diet

FIRE BITE

Flexible segmented exoskeleton protects internal organs

NEOTENIPEDE

Venomous claws for securing prey

DATA FILE
NAME Neoteni Centipede (or Neotenipede)
NA'VI NAME Pxayknam Txumtsin
TAXONOMY Aquapeda neotenica
HABITAT Rivers, lakes, and swamps.

Protective lid for bracts

Sensory tendrils

Gas buildup triggers spine projection

BRACT

PHALANXIA

The phalanxia is one of the most weaponized plants known to science. Its thick stem bears sensory tendrils and waxy bracts that encase heavy projectile spines. A second set of bracts, often mistaken for flower petals, functions as protective lids. Located between the primary and secondary bracts are tubular flowers where seeds are produced. The flowers are very difficult to reach without injury. Sensory tendrils that droop from under the primary bracts detect movement and eject sharp spines using gas that collects in bladders within the plant. These high-velocity darts inject a fast acting neurotoxin upon impact, which paralyzes within seconds, and kills in a few minutes. This ensures that the prey will drop in place and fertilize the soil within the grove of phalanxia. The toxin will kill smaller Pandoran creatures and, if shot precisely, can be deadly to larger animals and Na'vi. With precautions, however, the plant can be harvested. The Na'vi cut off the primary bracts to use their spines as darts and arrowheads.

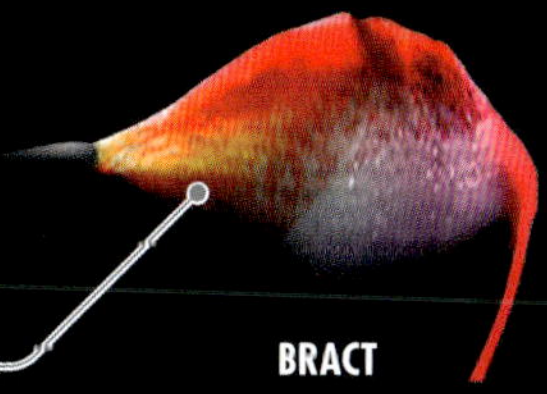

DATA FILE
COMMON NAME Phalanxia
NA'VI NAME Smaoe
TAXONOMY Phalanxia ferox. Root name means "armed military formation" and "fierce" or "thorny."
HEIGHT Up to 41 ft 9 in (4.5 m)
SPREAD 3 to 5 ft (1 to 1.5 m)
ECOLOGY Projectile spines prevent all but insects from eating the seeds.

THE RDA

THE RESOURCES DEVELOPMENT ADMINISTRATION (RDA) is a corporation with monopoly rights to all products shipped, derived, or developed from Pandora. These rights were granted in perpetuity by the Interplanetary Commerce Administration (ICA), with the stipulation that the RDA abides by a treaty that prohibits weapons of mass destruction and limits military power in space. However, these limits have gradually become more dynamic due to shifting circumstances. Following the RDA's evacuation from Pandora 15 years ago, the quality of life on Earth has significantly deteriorated—to the point where official analysis indicates that the human species can ultimately only be saved by mass migration to Pandora. Under this directive, the RDA has returned to Pandora to build Bridgehead as a foothold for full-scale colonization. It's no longer about profit margin for the RDA—it's about human survival.

BRIDGEHEAD

AFTER LITTLE MORE than a year of development, robotic "swarm assemblers" and autonomous vehicles achieved in a short time what manual labor would have taken years—transforming Bridgehead from a bare earth construction site into a thriving city. Defining the skyline are factories, refineries, and a powerplant that comprises an array of fusion reactors and cooling towers. Shipyards on the coast, protected by a seaward perimeter wall, are mass-producing SeaDragon ships, owing to the increasing demand for *tulkun amrita*, the youth serum that drives the interstellar economy. Large-scale 3D-printing gantries churn out the enormous components needed for the industrial megastructures envisioned for the future metropolis. Inflatable habs have given way to clean, modular dormitory stacks for thousands of workers, while giant video screens display news and morale-building encouragement in the burgeoning city center, shaping it into a more attractive place for residents. Bridgehead offers humankind a beacon of hope. The People of Earth can finally look to the stars for the chance to begin a promising new chapter for their future and their families. At least that's what the recruitment videos playing in the desperate dying slums of Earth will tell you.

RDA UTILITY VEHICLES
Rugged, all-terrain capability is a key feature across every vehicle type at Bridgehead, ensuring that drivers and their passengers move safely under any conditions.

UTILITY JEEP

AMBULANCE

NEWS BROADCASTING

Bridgehead is not only a center of industry but also a focal point of news, linking to a larger media and public relations apparatus connected to Earth. Camera crews record and upload video, viewable on screens and tablets and also relayed to Earth. With media services devoted entirely to Pandora due to high viewership ratings, new content is highly sought after. The recent invention of faster-than-light communication has transformed Bridgehead's media presence on Earth. Instead of having to obey Einstein's speed law, under which news from Pandora reached Earth 4.4 years later (traveling 4.4 light years in the process), quantum entanglement has enabled instantaneous news feeds to Earth.

HIGH-SPEED TRANSIT

Within a few decades after its start-up in the 21st century, the RDA developed an Earth-spanning, high-speed transit system that allowed the rapid transport of material, human labor, and robotic resources. It was critical to the support of megaprojects designed to shore up Earth's population centers against the devastating effects of climate change. This initiative led to Bridgehead's current network of maglev trains that require unobtanium for their continued operation.

THE RDA

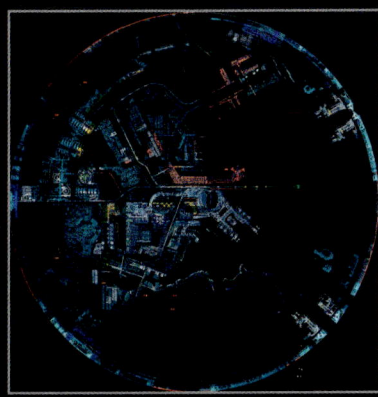

Digital map of Bridgehead.

A NEW COMMUNITY

Dormitory housing serves the majority of Bridgehead's residents. It is concentrated in two main zones that enable a short work commute and foster a sense of shared life around central community centers, indoor sports facilities, and semi-mercantile pedestrian zones. Large domes are being constructed to cover the lawns and mansions in the upscale section of town populated by RDA senior executives.

General Ardmore oversees all operations at Bridgehead.

UNOBTANIUM

Unobtanium does much more than just enable high-speed transit. Its superconducting properties allow global distribution of power without transmission losses, which is critical for Earth's entire energy grid. And it is fundamental to the magnetic containment cores of fusion reactors that power that grid. Unobtanium is also used in the magnetic containment of antimatter propellant tanks, which supply the antimatter-annihilation engines of the ISV's (Interstellar Vehicles) — the very basis of the interstellar economy.

FACT FILE

> The powerplant has a power output of 9 gigawatts, supporting industrial expansion and superluminal comms.
> In promotional videos, the RDA displays how Pandora has been civilized, reflected in the grandeur of Bridgehead. Jake Sully is depicted as a terrorist trying to stop human progress.

RDA CONSTRUCTION BLIMP

DATA FILE	
MANUFACTURER	RDA CON-DEV
MODEL	RDA Construction Blimp
NA'VI NAME	*Pxilìmpì*
HEIGHT	319 ft 7 in (97.4 m)
WIDTH	296 ft 1 in (90.26 m)
LENGTH	350 ft (106.68 m)
MAX. SPEED	75 mph (120.7 km/h)

THE RDA CONSTRUCTION BLIMP is a low-speed, heavy-lift platform. It consists of an orange working truss underneath two large silver gas envelopes, which produce considerably more lift than on Earth owing to Pandora's higher air density. It operates around Bridgehead, transporting large, prefabricated units of technology and architecture for installation in industrial plants and other facilities. The airship is also equipped to drop fire suppressant in emergencies, perform wide-range aerial spraying of herbicides and pesticides, and haul large animal carcasses from the kill zone, making it a true industrial workhorse.

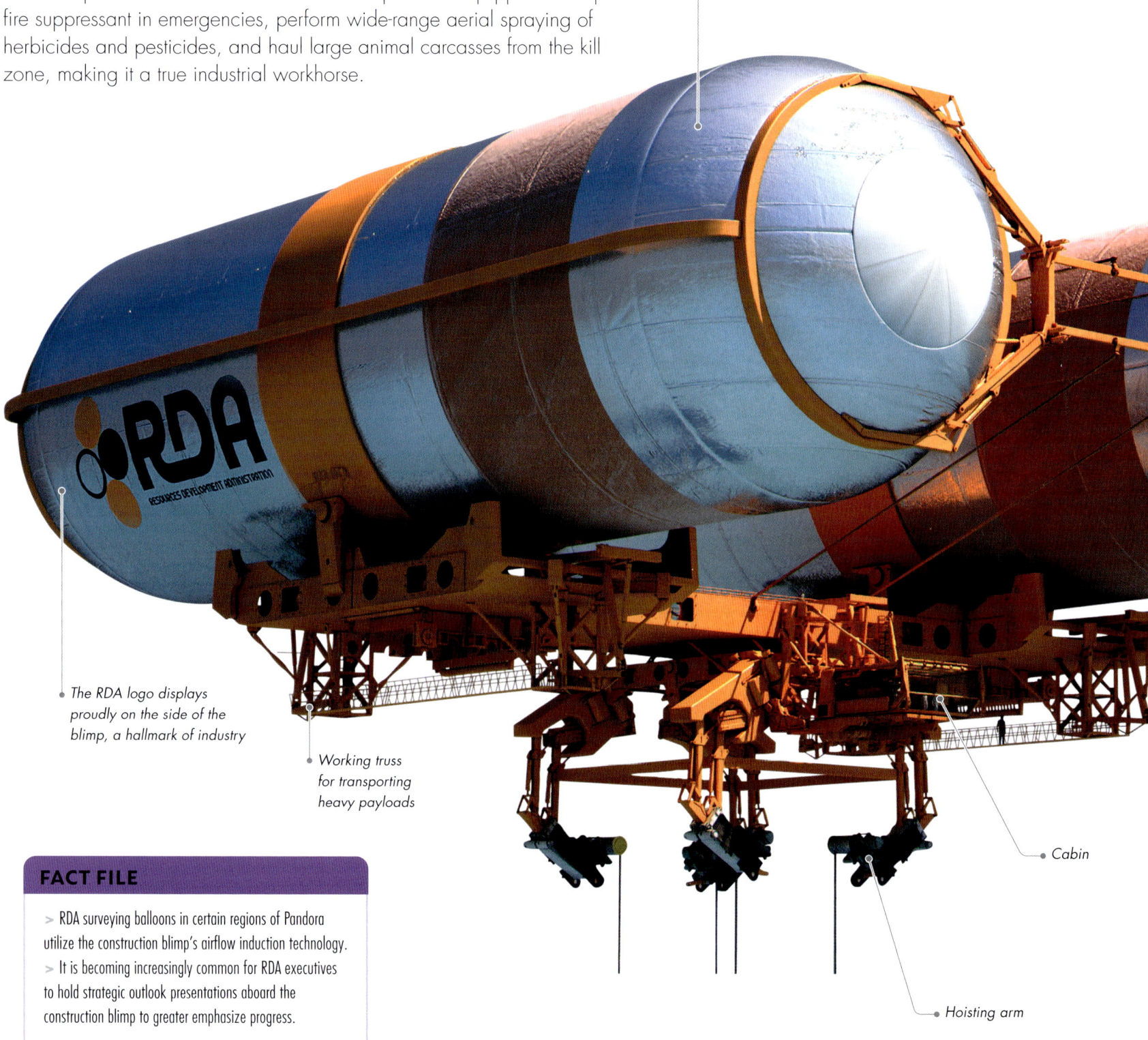

- Gasbag, also called an envelope
- The RDA logo displays proudly on the side of the blimp, a hallmark of industry
- Working truss for transporting heavy payloads
- Cabin
- Hoisting arm

FACT FILE

> RDA surveying balloons in certain regions of Pandora utilize the construction blimp's airflow induction technology.
> It is becoming increasingly common for RDA executives to hold strategic outlook presentations aboard the construction blimp to greater emphasize progress.

THE RDA

THE CABIN

The operator/utility cabin is designed to carry teams and small payloads and features a transparent floor that offers a panoramic view of the city below for monitoring and surveillance. The cabin also includes a navigation station, a pilot console, and a door leading to the maintenance catwalk for entering and exiting the vehicle.

RDA Administrator Parker Selfridge loves to take his morning coffee aboard one of the blimp airships, so he can take in the vista of the city.

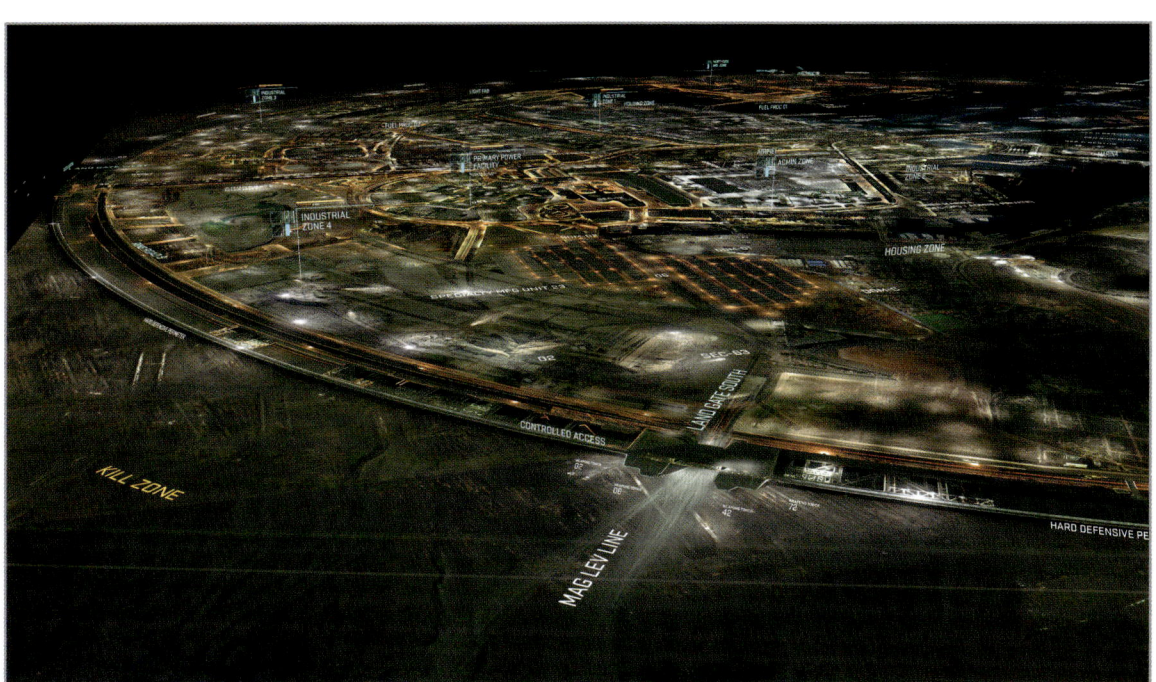

3D topography of Bridgehead at night as viewed from the blimp's navigation station monitor.

ADVANCED MAGNETIC TECHNOLOGY

Lacking any visible prop-rotors, the construction blimp maneuvers by two methods. For large distances, it uses airflow induction, channeling ionized air over and around the electomagnetized metallic skin of the gasbags to generate vectored thrust. For delicate maneuvering above Bridgehead, the blimp links to a grid of magnetic nodes embedded in the city's foundations made from the superconductor unobtanium. By establishing a matrix of varying magnetic polarities, the system creates differentials that allow the blimp to propel itself through the air by pushing from one magnetic node while being pulled to the next. Very precise positioning and station-keeping are enabled by this mag-grid tech. The RDA's maglev trains use the same technology when levitating across a magnetic track, but only move along a one-dimensional axis, whereas the blimp uses magnetics to achieve full three-dimensional movement and orientation control.

MANUAL PILOT

When not operating on autopilot, the pilot takes manual control of the blimp, typically for non-routine paths within Bridgehead or when traveling beyond the perimeter walls.

SCI-OPS COMPLEX

THE SCI-OPS COMPLEX stands as the pinnacle of biomedical research for all humanity. Equipped with state-of-the-art technology, it is dedicated to studying lush, mineral-rich Pandora, to enable human adaptation on the moon, and drive advances in a wide range of industries such as antivirals, biofuels, and pharmaceuticals.

The complex is situated in a standalone campus, protected by high-security measures to safeguard the classified work within. Inside, specialized laboratories, including the NeuroLab and the biomedical Scanner Lab, operate simultaneously. The Scanner Lab houses cutting-edge equipment for tissue and molecular sampling and analysis, highlighted by a high-end medical scanner. When it is discovered that Spider can breathe Pandoran air without a mask, a highly prioritized effort is launched inside the lab to understand the origins of the adaptation and replicate it—a task only the top scientists in the RDA can solve.

Personnel safety is a top RDA priority.

Main scanner area

The Sci-Ops complex at night.

THE RDA

Pipes for water and gases

Conduits for power and data

FACT FILE
> The Sci-Ops complex contains labs that are top secret, where only few have entered.
> Administrative benefactors believe the best way to tame Pandora is to better understand it through science.

Biomedical lab

Wrinkle-resistant RDA lab coat

A haptic glove that provides a tactile complement to holographic gestural interfaces.

NEUROBIOLOGIST

MYCELIAL ENDOSYMBIONT

Root transduction is a system of chemical signals exchanged among tree roots that regulates physiological processes between cells, such as nutrient sharing, immune response, growth, and reproduction. Mycorrhizae fungi or mycelium, which grows across tree roots enables this transduction. Both the trees and the fungus benefit from this association, which is called mutualism. Somehow, mycelium was able to colonize Spider, making cellular changes to his body, altering his blood chemistry, nervous system, lungs, and allowing him to breathe Pandoran air. Through mutualism, the mycelium acts as an endosymbiont; Spider and the fungus keep each other alive.

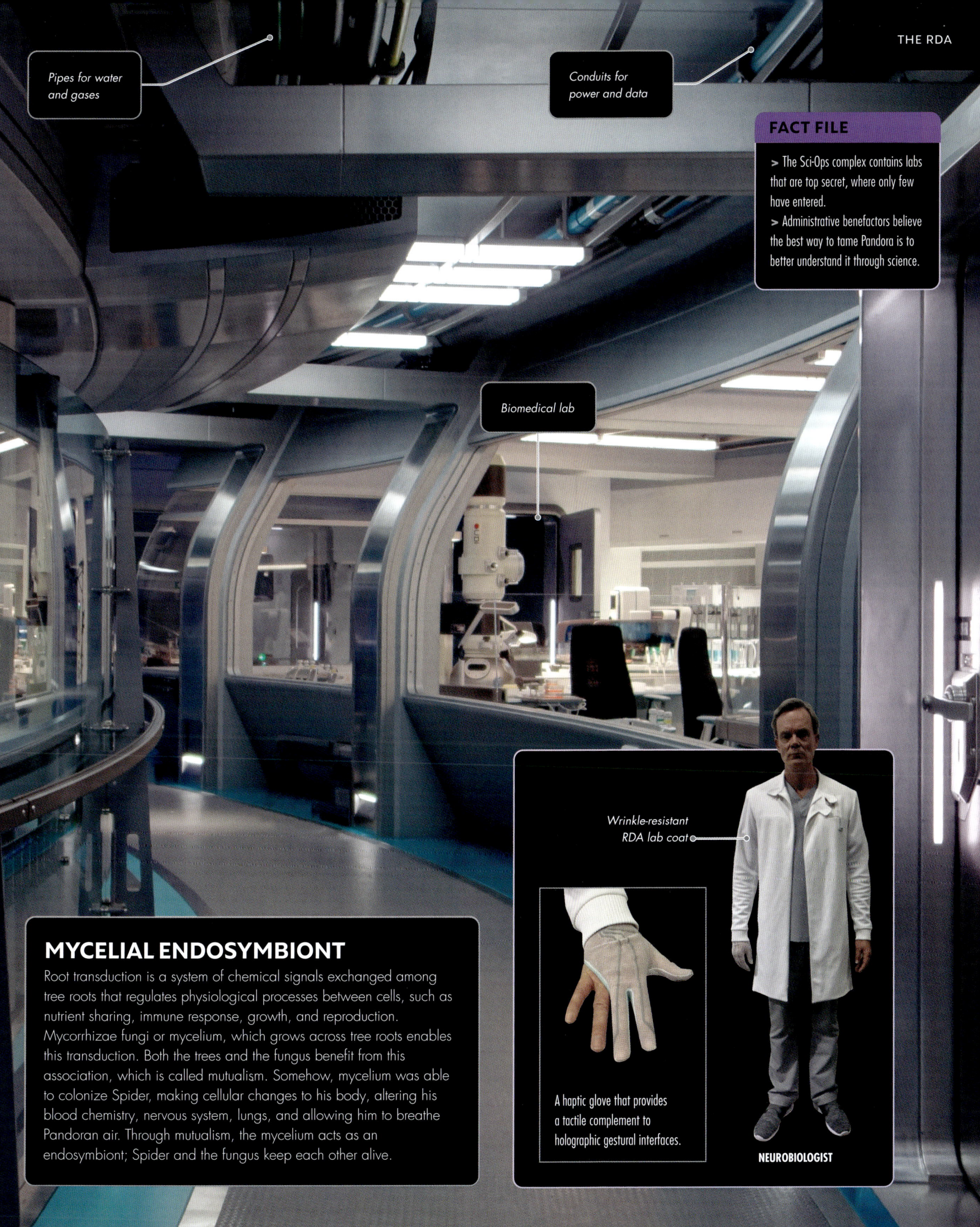

SCANNER LAB

IN THEIR RESEARCH to understand Spider's adaptation, scientists observe magnetic-resonance imaging from the scanner bed. By analyzing his blood and tissue samples, they seek to uncover how his respiratory cycle has changed, how his body is shedding or metabolizing the excess carbon dioxide of Pandora's atmosphere, and why his nervous system, modified by Pandoran mycelium, has extended into a neural interface or whip from the back of his skull—which the Na'vi call a *kuru*. In addition, the scientists view the endosymbiont's mycelial tendrils on Petri dishes to study its behavior. The combined results are examined via a hologram projected from a biomedical holotable. The mycelium is clearly still active within Spider's body, since his *kuru* is observed to be growing much faster than a normal Na'vi's.

ATMOSPHERIC CONTAINMENT

When running tests on Spider in the scanner bed, or on a treadmill that helps analyze how his body processes gases as he breathes, he is contained in a sealed plastic chamber that contains the Pandoran atmosphere to which he is now adapted. It is important to study Spider in his new native environment, so scientists must wear masks inside the chamber. Spider, however, is "amphibious"—he can breathe both Pandoran and human air with ease, further adding to the complexity and mystery of his transformation.

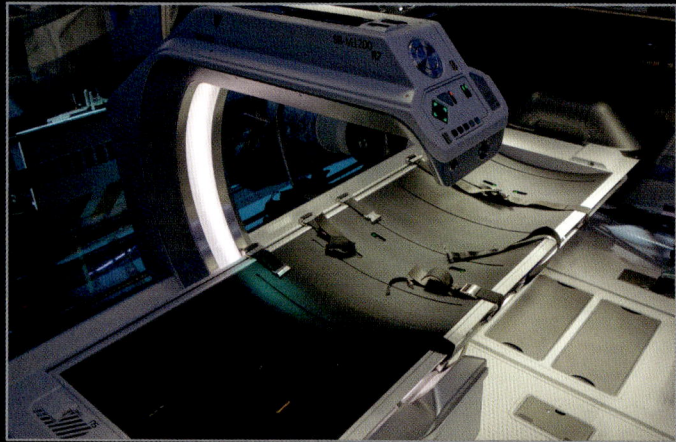

SCANNING BED

A high-end medical scanner, which superficially resembles a CAT scanner but is far more advanced, projects radiation from one end to a detector on the other. Using many small radiation emitters and imaging elements, the device performs sophisticated interferometry to produce volumetric models of bodily tissues of unprecedented precision and detail.

A holographic 3D scan displays the granular detail of Spider's cellular change captured by the scanning bed.

DATA COLLECTION

Scientists wear a thumb-size scanner that collects and transmits essential data from the environment to a chip card in their pocket—for faster processing and reduced error. Spreadsheets, graphs, and mind maps of the data are autogenerated by the time a scientist returns to their workstation.

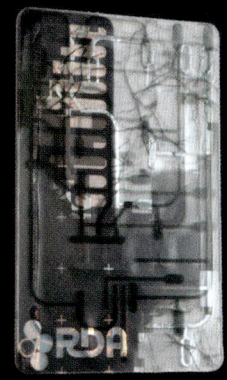
CHIP CARD

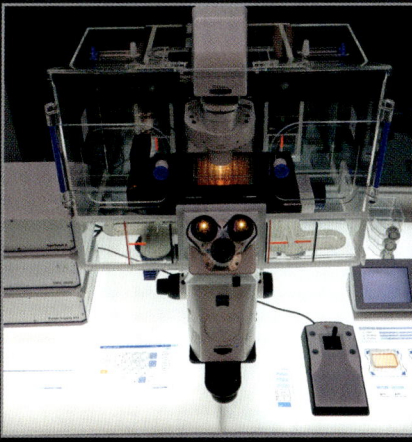
MICROSCOPE

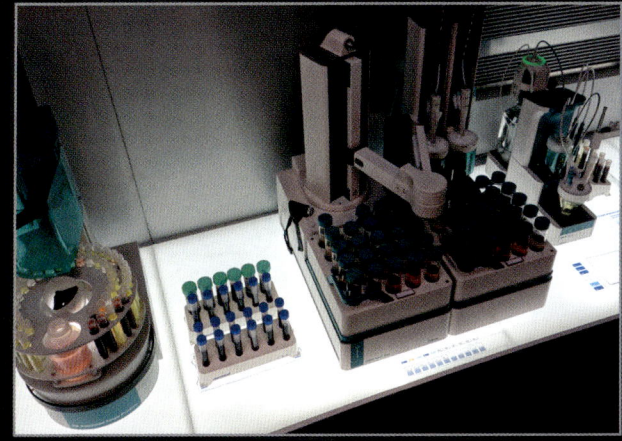
LIQUID-HANDLING ROBOTS

HOLOTABLE

RESTRAINED

Selfridge sees the future of the RDA in Spider—literally. He may not know how the endosymbiont living inside the boy allows him to breathe Pandoran air freely, but he understands the impact it could have on the company's bottom line.

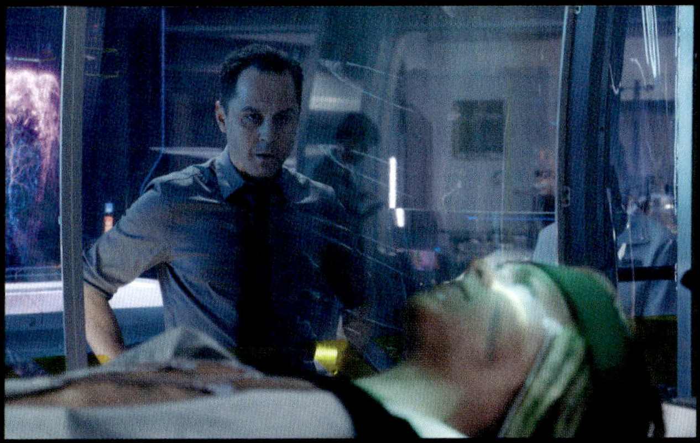

GENERAL ARDMORE

HAVING WON MANY BATTLES in her career, General Frances Ardmore is the best military tactician of her generation. She is a consummate professional soldier, who is as used to beltway politics as she is to combat. Her directive as Expeditionary Force Commander is clear: to secure Pandora for the mass colonization to come. To do that she must not only subdue the indigenous population, she must ensure the rapid scaling up of the extraction of Pandora's two most precious resources: *amrita*, the immortality drug, and unobtanium, vital to energy production and interstellar travel. These two resources provide the cash flow that makes colonization possible. Ardmore clashes with the Recombinant former Marine Colonel Quaritch over how this objective should be achieved. She is particularly frustrated by his repeated failures to capture Jake Sully, which have resulted in the loss of many Cet-Ops (Cetacean Operations) lives.

DATA FILE
FULL NAME Frances Ardmore
STATUS RDA Expeditionary Force Commander
AGE 53
BASE Bridgehead

INTERNAL STRIFE

Ardmore accuses Quaritch of getting "lost in the woods" when he conscripts the Ash People to help him track down Jake. The Ash People are an unknown quantity in Ardmore's eyes and can't be trusted. She believes Quaritch's Recom unit has served its purpose. It was an experimental program to begin with, and she's beginning to regret it as a bad idea. She can't let anything stand in her way. In these desperate times, she's got a mandate from the RDA to do whatever it takes to succeed.

- Four-star general insignia
- Security Operations (Sec-Ops) patch
- Personal tattoo (octopus)
- Z-33 standard firearm and holster
- Integrated knee pads

Ardmore is brusque and no-nonsense in her dealings with Quaritch's Recom.

THE RDA

FACT FILE

> Ardmore has been extremely effective in getting Bridgehead up and running, earning the respect of the RDA leadership and its shareholders.

> Ardmore fully appreciates the scientific, strategic, and financial opportunities that Pandora holds for the RDA.

CENTRAL COMMAND
Emerging from a CENTCOM vehicle, Ardmore counts on the Sec-Ops division to protect the RDA's security interests.

ARMORED COMMAND TRANSPORT

The Armored Command Transport (ACT) is a high-protection, all-terrain, six-wheel-drive transport for military officers and high-ranking RDA officials. This self-driving, automated vehicle has an onboard computer that manages system-control and driving functions, featuring a swivel camera and sensor mast for navigation. Despite its bulk, the ACT is highly maneuverable with omnidirectional wheel shift technology that allows for full 90 degrees rotation. It can drive straight and sideways and adapt its ride height for ground clearance and suspension travel for shock absorption and stability. It performs the trickiest maneuvers in dense urban or natural environments. General Ardmore uses the ACT for inspections through Bridgehead, checking on construction and perimeter defensive points, confident it can avoid collisions or endangering pedestrians.

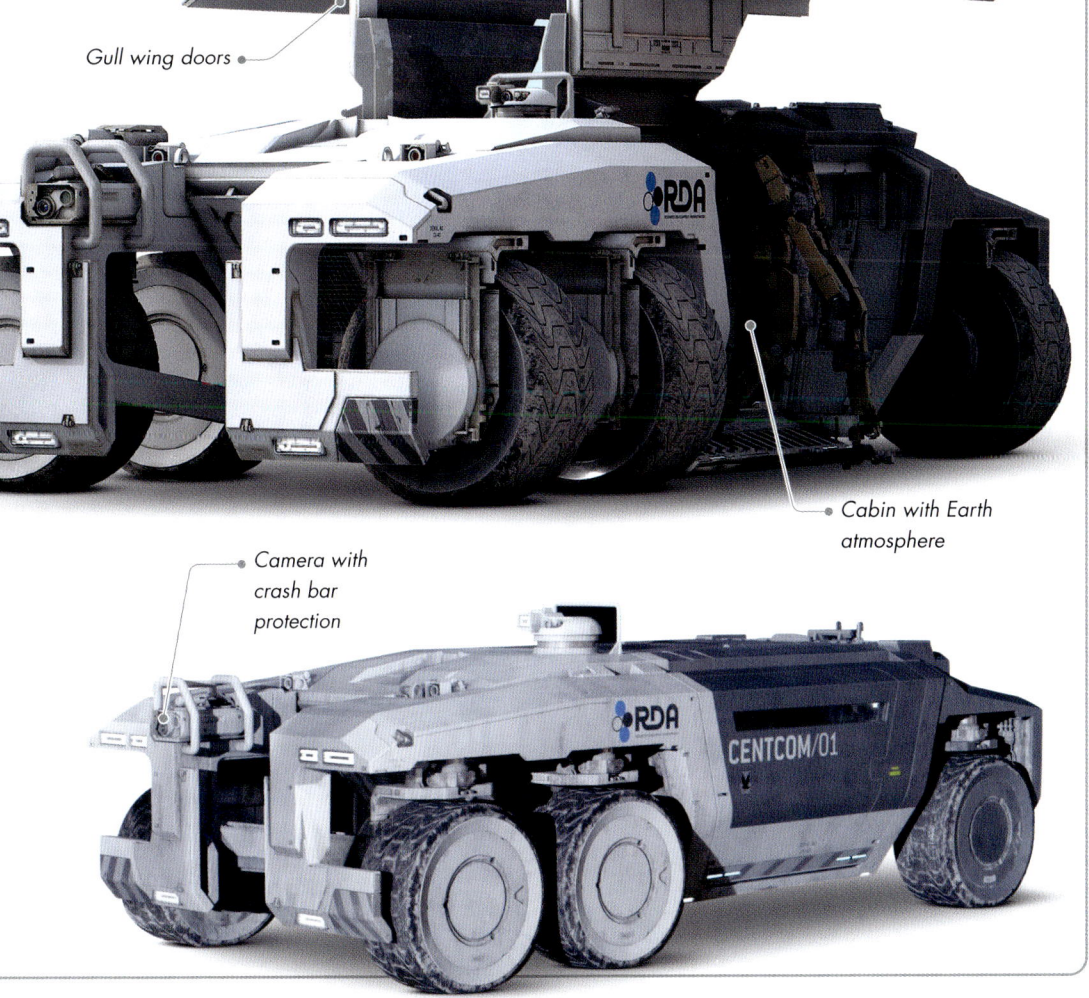

Gull wing doors

Cabin with Earth atmosphere

Camera with crash bar protection

COLONEL MILES QUARITCH RECOM

Having lost almost his entire Recom unit, as well as an RDA SeaDragon vessel and its crew in combat with Jake and Neytiri at Three Brothers Rocks, Quaritch's thirst for revenge is greater than ever. At the heart of his resentment is Spider's refusal to return with him to Bridgehead. The connection the Recombinant has with the boy he considers a son cannot be denied, especially since they are genetically bound by DNA. Now that Spider is hiding with the Sullys at the reef, Quaritch's aims—personal and professional—converge. The colonel knows he must stay focused on the mission he was brought 26 trillion miles for: a kinetic, hard-kill operation against Earth's most wanted enemy, Jake Sully. Only this time, he plans to break him.

Metal armbands

Quaritch thanks Spider for hauling him out of the sunken SeaDragon and saving his life.

CHAIN OF COMMAND

Quaritch is used to running the show, but under General Ardmore he is relegated to a hired gun. When he asks for more resources to capture Jake, Ardmore denies his request, citing too many assets have been wasted pursuing a fugitive gone to ground. When Quaritch discovers that Spider can breathe Pandoran air without a mask, he positions the boy as a bigger play. Quaritch is certain that capturing Spider will shatter Jake's resolve, force him to accept the RDA's inevitable victory, and sign a peace treaty, paving the way for humanity to permanently live and breathe on Pandora.

Dogtag of Miles Quaritch human, deceased

DATA FILE	
FULL NAME	Miles Quaritch
AFFILIATION	Phoenix Project
RANK	Colonel
BASE OF OPERATIONS	Bridgehead

THE RDA

POWER COUPLE
Quaritch encounters Varang, the mesmerizing *tsahik* of the Mangkwan, after her clan's attack on the Wind Trader flotilla and he works with Jake Sully to rescue Spider and the Sully kids. Quaritch and Jake are the first Sky People she has encountered, and they narrowly avoid death at her hands. He is strongly drawn to Varang, and grows convinced that she and her warlike anti-*Eywa* clan could be conscripted to form a native army against Jake. Quaritch offers Varang the scope, vision, and military means for a true escalation of force and power.

• Plate carrier

THE RECOM PROGRAM
Project Phoenix is perceived as a failure by General Ardmore owing to its high attrition rates, with 10 of 12 Recom operators neutralized in combat and no tangible results. The program engineered transgenic human/Na'vi hybrids with uploaded memories of seasoned Security-Operations (Sec-Ops) troopers able to endure the rigors of Pandora. While a key breakthrough is the Recoms' ability to bypass *Eywa*'s immune response, the costs outweigh the benefits. Ardmore is closely monitoring the remaining operatives in the field, evaluating whether long-term gains will justify present losses.

Deja Blu Recom patch •

The painted iconography depicts an erupting, black volcano. •

• Knapped crystal blade

MANGKWAN KNIFE AND SHEATH

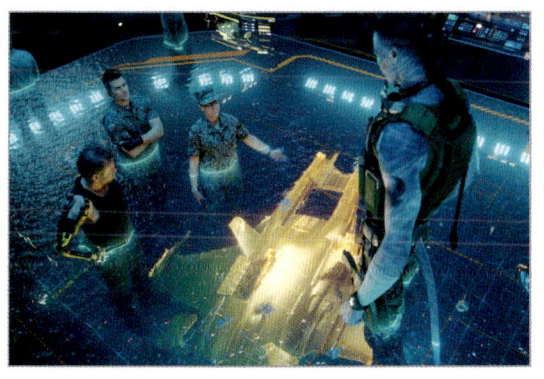

Recom M69-AR •

RDA *IKRAN* TACK
Designed by Quaritch, the ergonomic tack supports the *ikran* rider with textured grips and molle system for optimal load bearing.

CORPORAL LYLE WAINFLEET RECOM

STAUNCHLY LOYAL to Quaritch, Wainfleet relies on the colonel's disciplined leadership and is dedicated to meeting its standards while navigating unfamiliar terrain as a Na'vi/human hybrid. Following the deaths of his Recom unit, Wainfleet has learned not to underestimate the Sullys and Pandora, despite his hubris of military might and natural drive to dominate—a mistake his former self would have made without a second thought. He now acts on different instincts. His sniper training helps him to focus and steady his reactions to the environment around him, like a Na'vi. By remaining calm, collected, and more vigilant, he cultivates the skills and confidence needed to fulfill his duties in this new landscape.

Opens to activate holographic display

RECOM TABLET

Rubberized non-slip grip suitable for hot rainforest conditions

RDA TOMAHAWK

BUILDING A NETWORK

A standout figure at Bridgehead, Wainfleet leverages his position to grow his RDA network, sharing insights from the field with troopers and specialists while promising a sixpack of beer for any clear intel on Jake Sully's movements. The way he sees it, if the Na'vi can form an interconnected community, so can he. After all, he and the humans are already united in a common goal: a better life than awaits them on Earth.

DATA FILE
NAME Lyle Wainfleet
AFFILIATION Phoenix Project
RANK Corporal
BASE Bridgehead

THE RDA

Wainfleet is particularly skilled at long-range precision shooting.

• Burlap strips to break up Wainfleet's body outline

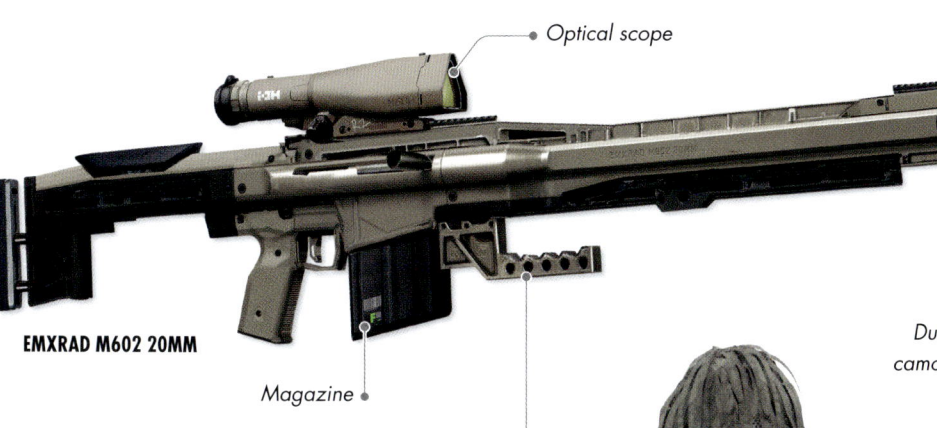

EMXRAD M602 20MM

• Optical scope
• Magazine
• Carry handle

• Dull color camouflage

SIGHT UNSEEN

Cloaked in a ghillie suit, Wainfleet blends into his surroundings—a silent killer, a ghost of Pandora, at one with his target. His lethal precision guarantees swift results, and he bears no regret over them, embodying the Recom purpose: becoming the weapon; the trigger; the change agent; a symbol of advancement.

FACT FILE

> Wainfleet is adapting to Pandora well; however, he has not assimilated the local Na'vi culture.
> With his unit gone, Wainfleet is learning to rely on his own resolve.
> Wainfleet is an expert sniper, trained in advanced weaponry, including an AMP Suit.

GHILLIE SUIT

PARKER SELFRIDGE

DISGRACED AFTER THE EXPULSION of the RDA in 2154, Selfridge, the former administrator of Pandora's on-world operation, returns to the moon 15 years later seeking to restore his reputation. Upon discovering Miles "Spider" Soccoro's ability to breathe Pandoran air without a mask, Selfridge is determined to capture and study the boy, in order to understand how this ability can be reverse-engineered for all humans. This would pave the way for humanity to make Pandora its new home.

DATA FILE
FULL NAME Parker Selfridge
STATUS Executive administrator
AFFILIATION RDA
BASE Bridgehead

A PERSONAL AGENDA

Selfridge encounters resistance from General Ardmore, who asserts that devoting valuable resources to the search for Spider diverts attention from more important and urgent objectives, such as establishing Bridgehead and harvesting *tulkun amrita* to pay for it. However, Selfridge can count on old alliances to uphold his agenda. With Recom Quaritch's collaboration, Selfridge hopes to earn back the favor of the RDA tenfold—and maybe, finally, be respectfully acknowledged by his father, the Chairman. He may even gain a nice homestead for himself on Pandora.

Expensive silk tie

Selfridge leads the applause that greets Jake Sully's capture by the RDA.

EARTH MEMORIES

The son of the Chairman of the RDA, Selfridge has made grave errors as an executive, and also in the eyes of his father. When he first returned home, he was viewed as a pariah, the black sheep of the family, farther from the center of power than ever. He was given one of the worst possible jobs: running the marketing for the RDA on Earth. It's a thankless task because Earth is a cesspit of squalor and disease. It is an overheated, violent, depleted, and dying world. Now back on Pandora, Selfridge makes it his quest to prove himself to his father and reinstate himself in the power elite by whatever means necessary.

FACT FILE
> If Selfridge can regain his RDA Chairman father's respect, he will become the most powerful person on Pandora.
> Earth is not a place Selfridge wants to return to, unless the Chairman makes him.
> Unctuous and arrogant, Selfridge is prone to using threatening and offensive language to achieve a desired result.

Like other Ops Center civilians, extraneous details such as shoelaces, belts, and bows have been removed from their attire to streamline human life off-Earth for peak efficiency

PERSONNEL EQUIPMENT

The true backbone of the RDA on Pandora lies within honest, hardworking professionals—from scientists and technicians to administrators and cooks. Each person has their own story for coming to the Pandoran frontier, yet they share a common theme: the pursuit of a better life through skill, grit, and the tools of their trade. Whether tracking data in the Ops Center or repairing machines in the Armor Bay, they work equipment that turns effort into progress—for the RDA and themselves. As they become essential parts of the system, their role earns them an increasing salary, allowing them to save for larger dorms, fresher foods, designer clothes, and next-gen tech, like personal holographic cameras. Comforts once out of reach on Earth are now attainable on Pandora—symbols, as the RDA describes it, of a shared experience that keeps them "Building Tomorrow" together.

Equipped with transparency mode

ACCOUTREMENTS
Office workers at Bridgehead wear small items day to day to pass through designated areas, whether for security purposes or as status indicators.

WORKSTATION CONSOLE
Each individual's workstation is designed for modularity and group dynamics, with clear lines of sight to neighboring displays. Depending on the operator's role, a workstation may also include custom hardware and software.

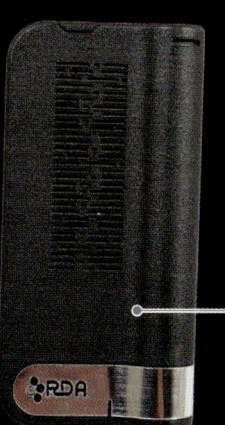

RFID TAG

Radio frequency ID tag worn near the collar or on the cuff for personal identification.

Often seen worn by management

BODY CAMERA

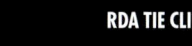

RDA TIE CLIP

HOLOGRAPHIC CAMERAS
Due to the prevalence of holographic displays, various recording methods are used to capture Pandora in the variety of ways that holograms allow, including 3D scanning for photogrammetry and telescopic lenses for high magnification.

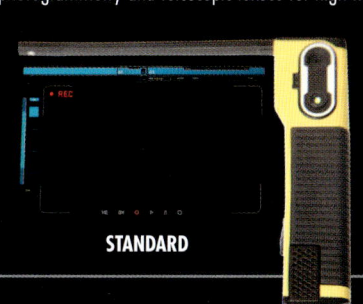

STANDARD

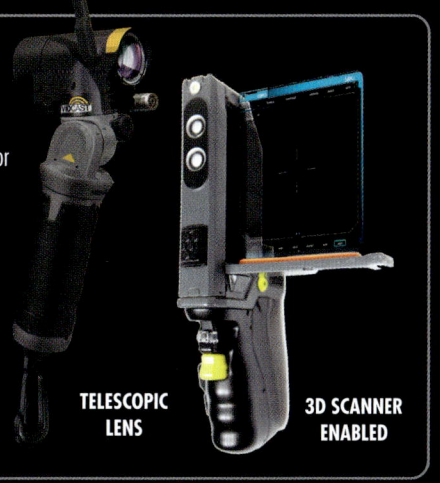

TELESCOPIC LENS

3D SCANNER ENABLED

TARMAC HELMET

HARD HAT

RDA logo

PROTECTION
Significant progress has been made in the construction of Bridgehead; however, it remains an active development zone, and caution is advised due to ongoing activity. Protective helmets are mandatory in several areas.

TOOL BELT
Worn by technicians across divisions such as Con-Dev and Sec-Ops, the tool belt is essential for quick, on-the-spot adjustments that require no power draw, especially when in the field or at an outpost, where resources are limited.

CAPTAIN MICK SCORESBY

REKNOWNED AQUATIC big-game hunter Captain Mick Scoresby has a harpoon to grind, having lost an entire crew at sea thanks to the provoked response of a rogue *tulkun*. Had Payakan not launched himself aboard the SeaDragon—prompting a full-scale battle between the RDA's vessels and Jake Sully and the Metkayina—Scoresby's crew would still be alive and he would not be falling behind on his quota for hunting *tulkun* and collecting the youth serum *amrita* from their brains. Symbolic of this defeat is his prosthetic right arm, which replaces the limb severed by Payakan. It serves as a constant reminder of unfinished business. Driven by ambition, Scoresby will stop at nothing to achieve vindication and vengeance.

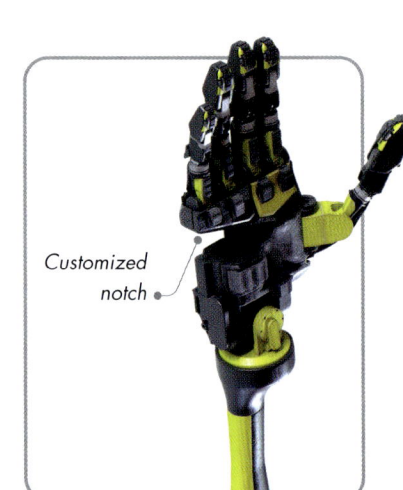
Customized notch

T-shirt of Scoresby's favorite baseball team on Earth

PROSTHETIC ARM

Scoresby's prosthetic X-Limb Ultra is made of carbon fiber, titanium alloy, and high-density polymer parts. It has been customized by Scoresby with an oversized hand to give him more control over maritime equipment—including his boat's throttle and harpoon gun—while wrangling heavy nylon towing lines that would damage an unprotected hand. At Scoresby's request, a notch in the palm allows him to hook onto mechanical levers and pull without letting go of a held object. His hand's grip has a crush force of 3,000 Newtons per square centimeter, enough to break human bone.

DATA FILE

FULL NAME	Captain Mick Scoresby
AFFILIATION	RDA
STATUS	Cet-Ops Big-Game Captain
SKILLS & PROFICIENCIES	Harpooning
BASE	Bridgehead

FACT FILE

> An expert hunter and harpooner, Scoresby is determined to meet—even exceed—his quota for collecting *tulkun amrita* and uphold his reputation as the greatest big-game hunter with the wildest, bravest crew.

> Scoresby prides himself on being able to use his prosthetic hand to pop open beer bottles and drink two at once.

Scoresby takes what he needs and leaves the rest behind.

DR. IAN GARVIN

INSPECTING THE SUNKEN WRECKAGE of the SeaDragon, RDA marine biologist Ian Garvin and his team discover new forms of algae. Although tasked with locating any signs of Jake Sully in the aftermath of the Three Brothers Rocks battle, he can't help but marvel at samples that extend the field of Pandoran oceanographic research. The RDA routinely demands his assistance with unsavory tasks, particularly hunting *tulkun*, under the threat of shutting down his research. Garvin reluctantly acknowledges the ethical dilemma of his compliance, rationalizing that it mitigates the number of needless *tulkun* deaths. However, he worries that rationalizing like this could desensitize him and prevent him from addressing his inner turmoil.

DATA FILE	
FULL NAME	Dr. Ian Garvin
AFFILIATION	RDA
PROFESSION	Marine biologist
BASE	Bridgehead

Scanner collects data from the environment and transmits it to a chip card

PATCHES

SPECIALIZATION — INSTITUTION

EXPEDITION — CLUB

DIVE KNIFE

Scuba-condusive chainmail for anti-bite protection

SCUBA OUTFIT

TULKUN ADVOCATE

As defense costs rise and the demand for *amrita* on Earth grows, so does the need to harvest the precious substance. Garvin is upset when he learns of Scoresby's plan to obtain several years supply of *amrita* in a single day by attacking pods of *tulkun* at the Tulkun Calf Communion. He knows this will lead to the slaughter of hundreds of the creatures as well as the attending Reef Na'vi. Garvin finally snaps, becoming an undercover *tulkun* defender and supporter. He resolves to do whatever it takes to sabotage the RDA's and Scoresby's efforts.

FACT FILE
> A lover and respecter of the ocean environment, Garvin feels guilt that his scientific expertise is being exploited by the RDA to hunt and harvest *tulkun*.
> Garvin longs for the time he was able to freely explore Pandora's oceans cataloguing scientific discoveries on a mobile catamaran-like lab vessel.
> He has a good understanding of *tulkun* culture and knowledge of their anatomy.

ASH ENCAMPMENT

THE MANGKWAN CLAN is recruited by Colonel Quaritch to establish a native army against Jake Sully. When Quaritch finally captures and brings Jake in, he arrives at Bridgehead with Varang and her warriors to set up operations. The Mangkwan are a macabre sight, a stark contrast to the image of order and control Bridgehead is trying to project. They raise a field version of the Ash village on the tarmac, rigging their yurts to light towers and overhead pipelines as they combine natural materials with stolen tarps and other RDA equipment. General Ardmore views the clan as invasive, but is willing to tolerate it until Jake is executed and any reprisals from the Omatikaya clan are suppressed.

PROJECTING FEAR

Varang becomes a rapid adopter of Bridgehead's industrial tech, such as lights, communications, and especially the RDA's munitions. For Varang and the Mangkwan, these weapons represent the ultimate abandonment of *Eywa* and the deity's sacred law prohibiting using metals from the ground. Using guns becomes a symbol of the clan's defiance and readiness to adopt new methods to destroy the old ways, leading the Mangkwan further down the conqueror's path. As Varang pulls the trigger on an assault rifle for the first time, she rejoices in her newfound ability to cause death and destruction. To project fear like never before. And when Quaritch gifts her with a flame-thrower, she feels a kind of divine rapture.

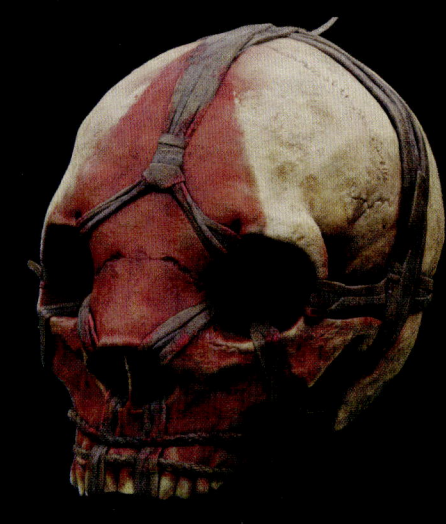

The Mangkwan have their own form of hacky sack, where a circle of players passes a skull to each other using their feet. The proportions of the skull look disturbingly human.

WEAPONS OF METAL

Quaritch equips the Mangkwan with various weapons, such as assault rifles, shoulder-fired missiles, RPG's (rocket-propelled grenades, flame-throwers, advanced military comms, and nightvision goggles. He then trains them to become the RDA's very own formidable Na'vi army.

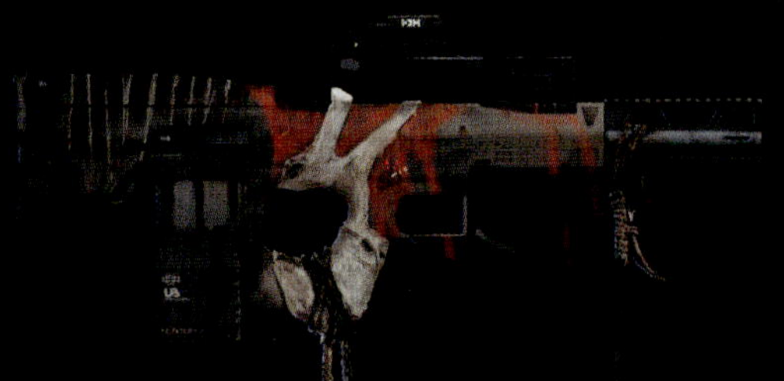

RECOM Y-70 BULLPUP

RPG LAUNCHER

Varang's yurt incorporates metals from Bridgehead.

CULTURAL RESPECT

All Bridgehead personnel are ordered to respect the autonomy of the Mangkwan, allowing them to maintain their customs and practices while operating on the base. This includes keeping a safe distance from spiritual dance ceremonies, and ritualistic sparring (which can result in the death of one of the combatants). Most importantly, personnel are strongly cautioned to avoid any interaction with the clan's *ikran*—there is no restitution agreement if a mount should snack on a human trooper or civilian.

FACT FILE

> The Mangkwan fetishize technology because it represents power. They throw away their bone piercings and replace them with metal posts and rings.
> Having zero appetite for RDA food, the Mangkwan hunt for their meals in the rainforest just outside the kill-zone.
> All the Mangkwan at Bridgehead are given IFF transponders, Identification/Friend or Foe badges that prevent them from being targeted by the automated defense turrets whenever they enter or exit the perimeter wall.

WILDLIFE CONTAINMENT UNIT

THE WILDLIFE CONTAINMENT UNIT is an artifact of the RDA Sci-Ops. The division's ongoing mission is to capture and study Pandoran wildlife, in some case sending the animals to Earth for examination and public display at RDA conservation centers such as the famous Pandora Park. The containment unit is a highly durable steel alloy and plexiglass box with a heavy-duty latching system and an integrated cargo chassis underneath for secure lifting and transport across various conveyances, including lowboy and flatbed transports. It is strong enough to contain the wide variety of Pandoran fauna up to and including a thanator. The containment unit is manufactured and maintained by RDA Con-Dev, but it is a custom application piece atypical for an organization that is usually focused on construction.

FACT FILE

> The wildlife containment unit's interior is fitted with an atmosphere-adaptation system to provide supplementary carbon dioxide for Pandoran lifeforms.
> Additional applications are currently being developed for the containment unit, including enhancing its protective capabilites for construction workers at off-site locations compromised by dangerous local wildlife.

Ventilation holes

Inside the WCU cage, Jake urges Quaritch to embrace the Na'vi Way and leave the RDA behind. However, the true nature of the world to Quaritch is not interconnection, but natural selection — the survival of the fittest — which he believes exists on Pandora just as it does on Earth.

DATA FILE

MANUFACTURER	RDA
MODEL	RDA WCU-500
AFFILIATION	RDA Con-Dev
SIZE	TBD
WEAPONRY	None

THE RDA

MISSION ACCOMPLISHED
Following the capture of Jake Sully, a WCU cage is prepared for his confinement, demonstrating its effectiveness at holding a powerful figure like *Toruk Makto*. By displaying its prized captive through its windows, the unit also serves a political propaganda purpose.

FLATBED TRANSPORT

The Con-Dev Flatbed Transport is an automated, self-driving transport platform used across Bridgehead to carry a range of loads, including heavy construction materials and construction bot assets. It is an all-purpose vehicle, capable of driving on roads, rugged dirt, and airfield tarmac. Its wheels can rotate 360 degrees, allowing precise movement in any direction at any time. The transport may be operated autonomously or remotely by a driver stationed at the Ops Center or positioned onsite using a portable wireless controller.

A flatbed hauls materials over dirt terrain.

Plexiglass window

Aluminum deck plates

Separates into two narrow transports

CON-DEV FLATBED TRANSPORT

LOWBOY TRAILER

The Con-Dev Lowboy Trailer can be paired with an RDA hauler to move a variety of large loads. It features a sophisticated locking mechanism for sliding and securing containers on the flatbed.

Load coupler

CON-DEV LOWBOY TRAILER

D-22 REMOTELY OPERATED BULLDOZER

If the RDA truly builds tomorrow, it starts the long, expensive, and politically sensitive process with one of its most basic tools—the heavy dozer. The D-22 is on the front line of the RDA's efforts to tame the Pandoran wilderness. It is designed to chew into the moon's topsoil to build roads for the expanding human presence, to assist heavy mining operations, flatten terrain for new construction sites, and dig holes for foundations. After decades of success in the last jungles of Earth, the D-22 required little or no adaptation for use on Pandora.

HIGH-TECH DESTROYER

An armored camera mast supports an array of cameras that gives the remote human operator many options for imaging the work site. In addition, forward sensor arrays under the front cowling, including ground penetrating radar and ultrasonic probes, scan ahead to determine soil depth, underlying geology, and the chemical components of the soil. The machine often operates in semi-autonomous mode, making decisions on its own while the human operator monitors its progress. Only in difficult terrain will the remote driver take over to directly operate the machine.

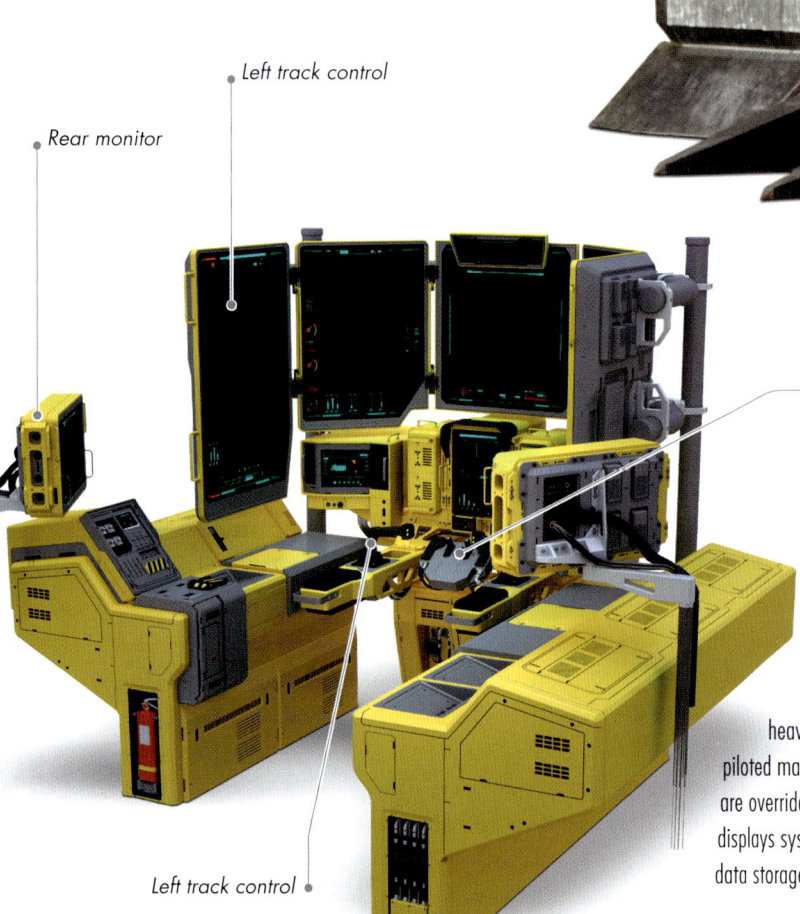

Armored camera mast

Rear monitor

Left track control

Front arm control unit

Left track control

CABIN CONSOLE
The dozer cab console is a heavy duty interface that can be piloted manually for when remote functions are overridden or non-operational. It also displays system diagnostics, GP map/radar, data storage, comms, and battery function.

DATA FILE	
MANUFACTURER	RDA
MODEL	D-22 ROB Series 2
NA'VI NAME	Tyom'akra ("Soil Eater")
AFFILIATION	RDA Con-Dev
SIZE	Wheelbase is 130 ft 3 in (39.7 m) long, (88 ft 5 in (26.93 m) wide, 43 ft 9 in (13.35 m) in height
WEAPONRY	None

THE RDA

The bulldozer's destructive capabilities prove as potent at Bridgehead as in the Pandoran rainforest.

FACT FILE

> The Na'vi consider the remotely operated bulldozer to be one of the great evils brought by human colonists and both fear and despise it.
> The vast majority of these vehicles is built on-world using 3D printing technology, utilizing in-situ resources.

SAFETY PROTOCOLS

There are several emergency features, including various procedures related to a broken blade, protocols regarding the discovery of archeological and paleontological finds, or the unexpected presence of a Na'vi. In such instances, the dozer's propulsion unit automatically shuts down as it awaits human guidance. To ensure efficient working methods, however, those safety features can be "tuned low" so that it takes a major disruption to trigger a shutdown. An operator can also manually access the interior cockpit and override the automated controls.

• Operates on treads made of permalloy

FRONT VIEW

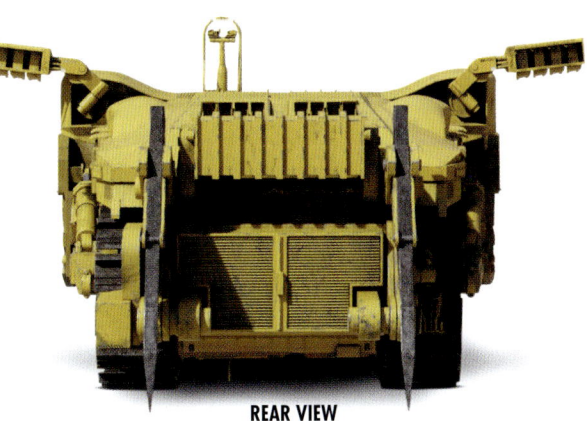

REAR VIEW

The D-22 has a front-mounted, huge single blade, and in the rear, a ripper attachment, both operated hydraulically. The machine travels on treads made of permalloy for a long operational life.

Access hatch leads to the engine bay and cabin.

119

MARITIME EXPANSION

The Factory Ship towers above all vessels in the Cet-Ops fleet.

THE RDA ACKNOWLEDGES the stunning overthrow of a Cet-Ops (Ceteacean Operations) hunt at Three Brothers Rocks by Jake Sully, resulting in a SeaDragon lying wrecked at the bottom of the ocean with the loss of all crew. Instead of phasing back its operations, the corporation has evaluated the extent of the damage and, after internal review, decided to continue Cet-Ops hunting of *tulkun* unabated. Management cites the growing market for *amrita* and the need to show strength in the face of terrorism. The RDA is taking corrective action by enhancing defense systems and refining crisis management strategies. They upgrade to new weaponry, including the addition of the G-37 30mm Manned Air Defense Turret. The RDA also expands its fleet with a massive Factory Ship, which greatly increases their *tulkun* harvesting capability. Cet-Ops is committed to delivering gains that will continue to improve the quality of life at Bridgehead.

SeaDragon fan cowl

G-37 30MM AIR DEFENSE TURRET
Two vertically-stacked 30mm cannons fire exploding rounds with barometric fuses against airborne assailants. The Factory Ship has four G-37 gun turrets.

Picador short-range patrol boat

THE RDA

FACTORY SHIP

GARUDA

CRAB SUIT

SEADRAGON

DRAGON

KESTREL

SCORPION

SEAWASP

SAMSON

MATADOR

PICADOR

MAKO

ATV

GAV

TASK FORCE

The RDA continues to build out its task force by air, land, and water — every element of which, in one way or another, supports Cet-Ops. Whether through security, dockside loading, or maritime airdrop, the RDA's formidable fleet functions as a virtually unstoppable unified system.

TORPEDO SLED

On support ships like the Factory Ship and SeaDragon, wheeled sleds are used to transport torpedos safely to hunting vessels or aircraft.

Lightweight torpedo

FACTORY SHIP

LIKE AN AIRCRAFT CARRIER, the Factory Ship is a true mothership. The high-tech SWAQH vehicle (Small Waterplane Area Quad Hull) boasts a sixfold- greater processing capacity for harvesting *tulkun* than the SeaDragon. The need for this technological advance arose as the youth serum *amrita*—derived from *tulkun* brains—became the single most important source of revenue from Pandora. The windfall from *amrita* on Earth has allowed the rapid expansion of the colonizing efforts. While initially the SeaDragon met established quotas, its hunting capacity exceeded its processing ability, as it could only target one *tulkun* at a time when encountering pods of several animals, resulting in fewer kills. In response, the RDA built the Factory Ship, a larger platform that supports more kill boats like the Matador, Picador, Mako, and Crab Suit, and processes multiple *tulkun* simultaneously, greatly increasing fleet capacity and efficiency. The Factory Ship is specifically designed to handle the payload of five SeaDragons and serve as the flagship of the hunting armada.

FACT FILE
> There are approximately 200 crew members, just under half of whom are dedicated to the smaller hunting vessels.
> The crew stay out on the Pandoran ocean for months at a time.
> *Amrita* is in great enough demand on Earth to warrant a second Factory Ship. This product is taken by only the wealthiest humans to stop the aging process.
> There is only one Factory Ship active at sea. A second ship is under construction at the Bridgehead dry dock printing and assembly facility.

RED FOR DANGER
The exterior of the Factory Ship is painted with industrial red anti-fouling paint, for visibility to other vessels and to prevent marine growth on the hulls. It stands on four independent hull sponsons, hidden below the waterline, where propulsion systems are located. These are connected to the main body of the ship by slender struts that cut efficiently through the water when the ship is in its higher-freeboard transit mode.

UTILITY CRANE
Multiple giant cranes are for cargo onloading and resupply.

EMERGENCY ESCAPE VEHICLE
A lifeboat that drops from the side of the ship for emergency evacuation of the crew. Each one accommodates 50 people.

MAIN HELIPAD
The Factory Ship has three helipads. The main helideck can accommodate vehicles up to a C-21 Dragon gunship, while the secondary helipads—one situated on the stern and one on the aft port side—are for Sea Wasp and Kestrel gunships.

FACTORY SHIP BRIDGE
This command center is a mobile Ops Center of the sea. It contains an extensive array of visual displays, a spacious holotable, a large number of operators, technicians, and two pilots for greater situational awareness and task distribution. The bridge's wraparound windows give the operators a panoramic view, while side airlock doors lead to bridge wings, an elevated catwalk, and the main helipad.

THE RDA

RAMPING UP THE KILLING

Each side of the ship has two deck ramps: one dedicated to harvesting *tulkun* and deploying and recovering Picadors, and the other serving as a launch dock with davits for Matadors. It can be reconfigured to an extra harvest ramp if needed. A rear ramp duplicates the boat deployment and *tulkun*-processing capabilities seen on the SeaDragon. The extra wide forward ramp at the bow of the Factory Ship serves for harvesting *tulkun* and deploying Crab Suits on a massive scale. This ramp is the largest in the fleet and can handle elder *tulkun* as long as 377 ft (115 m). Elder *tulkun* are a special boon to the RDA, as the leviathan's brain will generate voluminous amounts of *amrita*.

Engineered to harvest *tulkun* day and night.

The RDA is convinced that the Factory Ship leads the way to greater gains.

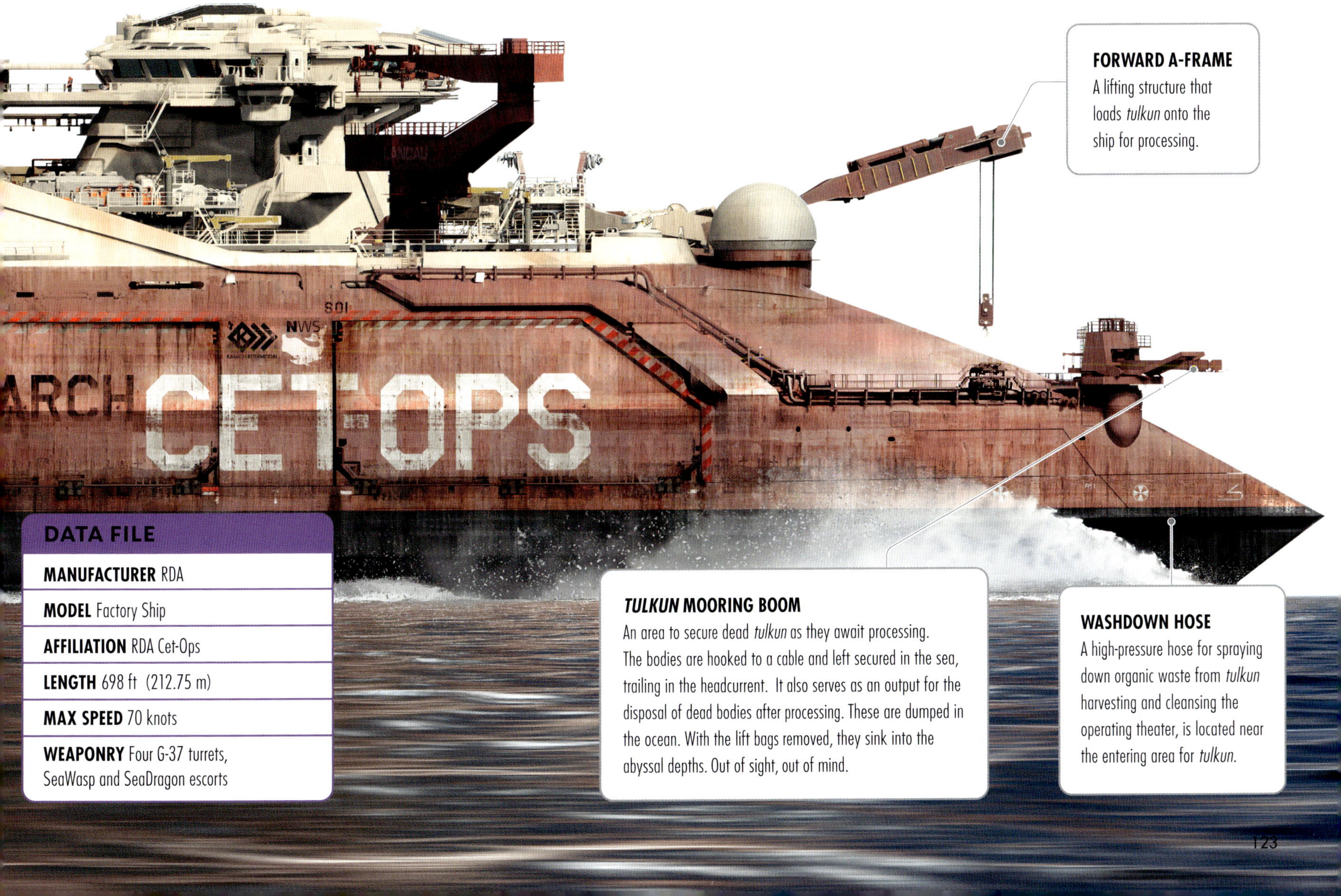

FORWARD A-FRAME
A lifting structure that loads *tulkun* onto the ship for processing.

DATA FILE

MANUFACTURER RDA

MODEL Factory Ship

AFFILIATION RDA Cet-Ops

LENGTH 698 ft (212.75 m)

MAX SPEED 70 knots

WEAPONRY Four G-37 turrets, SeaWasp and SeaDragon escorts

***TULKUN* MOORING BOOM**
An area to secure dead *tulkun* as they await processing. The bodies are hooked to a cable and left secured in the sea, trailing in the headcurrent. It also serves as an output for the disposal of dead bodies after processing. These are dumped in the ocean. With the lift bags removed, they sink into the abyssal depths. Out of sight, out of mind.

WASHDOWN HOSE
A high-pressure hose for spraying down organic waste from *tulkun* harvesting and cleansing the operating theater, is located near the entering area for *tulkun*.

HOLOTABLE

THE HOLOTABLE on the Factory Ship is a console-style holographic volume based on the same technology as the holofloor at the Bridgehead Ops Center, an immersive, walk-in environment with a grid of holographic projectors arrayed beneath the glass floor. Users engage with holograms for spatial planning and data mapping, leveraging them as tools for collaborative communication among individuals and groups. The technology allows for teams to visibly share and manipulate digital models, image files, and datasets in an organized format that is layered, linked, and intuitively understood, optimizing what humans have done for millennia: responding to information in 3D space. In a lab context, RDA technicians use holograms to better understand and exploit the amazing science of Pandora.

ADVANCED WARFARE

The RDA Sec-Ops use holograms to simulate combat scenarios, including rehearsing decision-making with real-time historical feedback, observing behavioral patterns, and recording outcomes for future reference and implementation in the field. During combat, the hologram displays the theater of engagement. The air traffic layer shows 3D positions of aircraft transponders, linked through chains of command. The ground layer is a composite of satellite and aerial imagery in infrared, mapped over a 3D terrain model. Infrared imaging also reveals enemy positions, including those beneath the ocean surface.

Open area provides clear line of sight to console displays

3D terrain model

FLOOR SPACE
At a holographic volume measuring 30 ft (9.1 m) in length, 24 ft (7.3 m) in width, and 18 ft (8.5 m) in height, the Holofloor can occupy a large team, including Recom-size personnel.

Primary target highlighted in yellow

INDEX

A
akula 39, 44, 50, 54, 57
amrita 53, 96, 112, 113, 120
anklets 21, 30
Ao'Nung 38, 44, 45
Ardmore, General Frances 104–05, 106, 107
armbands and arm wraps 12, 14, 17, 18, 20, 21, 27, 31, 106
   Mangkwan 84
   Metkayina 16, 38, 42, 44
   Omatikaya 27
   Tayrangi 33
   Tlalim 60, 61
armguards and gauntlets 15, 27, 32, 85
Armored Command Transport 105
Ash People *see* Mangkwan
Ash Encampment 114–15
Ash Village 78–81, 86
Augustine, Dr. Grace 13, 15, 16

B
ballista 67
bangles 60
beads and beading 17, 20, 25, 31, 32, 45, 69, 86
bioluminescence 16, 50, 54, 55, 58
bolas 80
bows and arrows 14, 67, 80, 81
   war bow 15, 19, 42
braiding 12, 15, 27, 39, 43, 44, 68
breathing equipment 30, 31
Bridgehead 22, 96–97, 106, 111
   Ash Encampment 114–15
   Sci-Ops Complex 100–01, 116
buugeng sticks 84

C
Calf Communion Ceremony 46, 113
caves 47
centipedes 92, 93
Cet-Ops (Ceteacean Operations) 120–21
chest guards 38, 41, 44, 45
chest pieces 16, 60, 61
cloaks and capes 21, 30, 39, 42, 60, 66, 68, 69, 85
collars 68, 85
Coming of Age Ceremony 36, 37, 41, 43, 44
Construction Blimp 98–99
Cove of the Ancestors 16, 41, 46–47, 48
Crab Suits 45, 54, 121, 123
cummerbunds 27, 61, 68

D
D-22 Remotely-Operated Bulldozer 118–119
direhorse toy 25
drums 24, 37, 61, 64, 80
dust pouch 85

E
earrings 81, 84
Eywa 9, 16, 26, 76, 84

F
Factory Ship 122–23
fire suppression bag 66
First Breath Ceremony 36
fishing gear 37
Flux Devil 48–49
food and food preparation 24, 63, 79, 80, 115

G
Garvin, Dr. Ian 113
ghillie suit 109
goggles 30
gondolas 64–65, 66, 73, 88
gourds 61, 64, 80
great leonopteryx 12, 70
guns 12, 109, 114, 120
G-37 30mm Air Defense Turret 120

H
hair adornments 17, 27
headbands and headpieces 26, 33, 42
High Camp 12, 16, 20
holographic cameras 111
Holotable 124–25
Hometree 22, 76, 77, 78

I
ICA (Interplanetary Commerce Administration) 94
IFF (Identification/Friend or Foe transponder) 107, 115
Ikeyni 32–33
ikran 15, 20, 29, 33, 61, 64, 67, 77, 115
   riding equipment 12, 18, 24, 80, 107
ilu 21, 43, 45

K
Kiri 13, 16–17, 31, 45
knives
   Ikenyi 32
   Mangkwan 80, 81, 85, 107
   Metkayina 18, 39, 41, 43, 44, 45
   Omatikaya 21, 27, 31
   Sully family 12, 14, 16, 18, 20, 21
   Tlalim (Wind Traders) 67
kuru 21, 26, 32, 61, 69, 78, 80, 84, 85, 86
   connection (*tsaheylu*) 43, 66, 72
   grown by Spider 31, 102

L
leaf adornments 17, 21, 42, 68
leggings 33
leg guards 27
Lo'ak 14, 18–19, 42, 43, 44
loincloths 14, 20, 26, 33, 43, 44, 81

M
maglev train 96, 99
Mako submersible 54, 121, 123
Mangkwan clan 9, 12, 67, 76–77, 114–15
   weapons 80–81, 84, 85
medusoids 60, 62, 66, 70–71, 80
Metkayina clan 8, 13, 15, 20, 36–37, 42
mining operations 22, 118
Mo'at 17, 26–27
music 60, 61, 64
mycelium 17, 28, 31, 102

N
nalutsa bull 32
necklaces and chokers 14, 17, 18, 26, 31, 44, 69, 81, 85
Neteyam 12, 14, 15, 18
Neytiri 12, 13, 14–15, 28, 40, 41
nightwraith 88–89

O
Olangi clan 29
olo'eyktan and *olo'eykte* 13, 22, 27, 32, 64, 68, 84
Oma 31
Omatikaya clan 8, 22–24, 33
   toys 25
Outriders 12, 64

P
Pandora 8–9
   ocean 50–51, 120–21
Patel, Dr. Max 29

Payakan 19, 42, 43, 53, 112
Peylak 12, 60, 68–69
phalanxia 93
piercings 76, 81
Polyphemus 8
Pril 39, 41
Project Phoenix *see* RDA, Recom Program

Q

Quaritch, Colonel Miles (Recom) 13, 30, 31, 48, 87, 104, 106–107, 114

R

RDA (Resources Development Administration) 9, 13, 22, 53, 94–95
   biomedical research 100–03
   transport 96, 97, 98–99, 105, 117
   Recom (Recombinant) Program 107
Riku 78
Ronal 17, 38, 40–41, 42
Rotxo 45

S

scarification 76, 84
Sci-Ops 100–01, 116
Scoresby, Captain Mick 112, 113
SeaDragon 12, 15, 19, 30, 42, 48, 106, 113
sea caves 47
Selfridge, Parker 110
skimwing 37
skirts 40, 60, 68
Socorro, Miles *see* Spider
songcords 13, 14, 15, 17, 19, 20, 31, 33, 39, 43, 45
spears and halberds 40, 67, 68, 78, 81
Spellman, Dr. Norm 28–29
Spider 12, 16, 20, 21, 28, 29, 30–31, 48, 102, 103, 106
Spirit Tree 16, 46
Sully, Jake 12–13, 38, 39
swamps 90–92

T

Ta'nok 53
Tarsem 27
tattoos 36, 40, 41, 43, 85, 104
Tayrangi clan 32, 33
tetrapterons 88
thanator 14, 85, 116
Three Brothers Rocks 15, 40, 42, 106, 112, 120
Three Laws 9

Tlalim clan 8, 60–64 also see Wind Traders
Tonowari 14, 38–39, 42
toruk 12, 13, see also leonopteryx
   toy 25
Toruk Makto 12, 13, 38
totems 45, 68, 78, 86, 87
toys 25
Tree of Souls 16
trinkets 60, 62
tsaheylu 43, 66, 72, 80
tsahik 17, 26, 40, 84
Tsireya 38, 42–43
tsyong 43, 54–55, 59
tuff 77
Tuktirey (Tuk) 15, 20–21, 25
tulkun 19, 36, 38, 41, 42, 43, 50, 120
   Council of Elders 52–53
   hunted by RDA 113, 122–23
   toy 25

U

unobtanium 46, 97, 98

V

Varang 84–87, 88, 107, 114
volcano 74, 75, 76, 77, 84

W

Wainfleet, Corporal Lyle (Recom) 108–109
war paint 15, 32, 80
water drum 37
weapons 67, 80–81, 84
weaving 21, 24, 36, 37, 86
Wildlife Containment Unit (WCU) 116–17
windbuys 66, 72–73
Wind Traders (Tlalim clan) 8, 12, 36, 60–63, 68
   gondolas 64–66, 72, 73
   market 62–3
   weapons 67
wrist cuffs, wraps, and bracelets 17, 19, 20, 68

Y

yurts 78, 86–87

Z

zukzuk 50, 56

TUKTIREY

SENIOR EDITOR
Alastair Dougall
PROJECT ART EDITOR
Jon Hall
DESIGN
Lauren Adams
PRODUCTION EDITOR
Marc Staples
SENIOR PRODUCTION CONTROLLER
Mary Slater
MANAGING EDITOR
Emma Grange
MANAGING ART EDITOR
Vicky Short
ART DIRECTOR
Charlotte Coulais
PUBLISHER
Paula Regan
MANAGING DIRECTOR
Mark Searle

First published in Great Britain in 2025 by
Dorling Kindersley Limited
20 Vauxhall Bridge Road,
London SW1V 2SA

The authorised representative in the EEA is
Dorling Kindersley Verlag GmbH. Arnulfstr. 124,
80636 Munich, Germany

Copyright © 2025 Dorling Kindersley Limited
A Penguin Random House Company
10 9 8 7 6 5 4 3 2 1
001–348769–Dec/2025

© 2025 20th Century Studios.
All Rights Reserved.

All rights reserved.
No part of this publication may be reproduced, stored in or introduced into a retrieval system, or transmitted, in any form, or by any means (electronic, mechanical, photocopying, recording, or otherwise), without the prior written permission of the copyright owner. No part of this publication may be used or reproduced in any manner for the purpose of training artificial intelligence technologies or systems. In accordance with Article 4(3) of the DSM Directive 2019/790, DK expressly reserves this work from the text and data mining exception.

ISBN 978-0-2417-3314-1

Printed and bound in China

www.dk.com
www.avatar.com

ACKNOWLEDGMENTS

DK would like to thank the following for their assistance in making this book: James Cameron, Jon Landau, Rae Sanchini, Joshua Izzo, Reymundo Perez, Maria Battle Campbell, Jamie Landau, Ben Procter, Dylan Cole, Deborah L. Scott, Joseph C. Pepe, Zachary Berger, Hana Scott-Suhrstedt, Shealyn Biron, Carrie Hollinger, Aashrita Kamath, Brad Elliot, Molly Berg, Jeffrey Reeves, Paul Frommer, Peter Litvack, Joy Chase, John Hernandez, Edu Black, Dean Lewandowski, Jessica Pollack, Jacqi Dillon, Colbert Fennelly, Chris Cornejo, Summer Benton, Billy Barnhart, Chikako Hoffman, John Manko, Lisa Fitzpatrick, Danny Shelby, Anneke Suyderhoud, Stephanie Nelson, Samara Poche, Madeline Heyman, Alexandria Cowell at Lightstorm Entertainment; Wētā FX; Wētā Workshop; Industrial Light & Magic; Legacy Effects; Nicole Spiegel at Disney, Lauren Adams for layout design; Julia March for the index.